Purpose Over Position is an absolute game changer. Vad Lee does an amazing job showing us how God can provide us with our best blessings, even from what we perceive to be our worst situations. Take on this journey with Vad, and transition from your position to your purpose.

—**Eric Mac Lain, ESPN and ACCN College Football Analyst, Former Clemson Football Team Captain**

In *Purpose Over Position*, Vad shares practical and authentic wisdom that is crucial for living a life of purpose. Using the highs and lows of his athletic career, Vad gives tips critical for spiritual growth and becoming who God has intended you to be. No matter your athletic prowess, this book will help get you to the top of your game.

—**Pete Hardesty, co-author of Amazon No. 1 bestseller** *Adulting 101*

Purpose Over Position is a must-read! Vad brilliantly uses his success and adversity from his playing to career to eloquently show the reader the power of trusting in the Lord! Vad's ability to show his vulnerability and be transparent with the reader is truly remarkable. This book will not only inspire you, but it will also challenge you to walk in your purpose!

—**Arthur Moats, Former Pittsburgh Steelers LB, author** *Moats Theory of Life,* **The Arthur Moats Show Podcast**

National champion as a youngster, state champion and All American quarterback as a teenager, college superstar, young husband, father and ministry leader; Vad Lee has been touched by the Lord to share some of life's greatest lessons. Vad takes the reader from the highest highs of athletic stardom to the lowest lows of a dream-ending injury and the accompanying behind- the-scenes doubt, wonder, and darkness. As Vad shares his life's journey in his first book, he offers wisdom beyond his years as he frames and reframes his career and life experiences with the eternal perspective of scripture, rather than social media and popular/modern culture.

Looking back on my life, I only wish I would have had access at a younger age to the biblical truths Vad shares in POP. Readers with a heart to seek the Lord's perspective on life's journey will be blessed."

—**Scott Stankavage, QB UNC/Denver Broncos/Father of seven/author** *THE QB MENTOR* **and** *GOD ALWAYS HAS A PLAN*/**Leukemia and bone marrow transplant survivor**

I've had the sincere pleasure of knowing Vad and his family for many years. His story personifies persistence. As great a record-setting quarterback as he was on the field, he's an even better person with a story that can inspire us all.
—LeVelle Moton, NC Central Head Basketball Coach

In this gripping account of his most difficult moment, Vad Lee uses this experience to lift his life above his position as the QB of one of the most potent offenses in college football to a level of purpose that only God could have created.
—Derrick Moore, Director of Character Development for Georgia Tech Football, Author of *The Great Adventure* and *It's Possible*

Vad Lee is a great example of someone walking with God through the ups and downs of life. His example of going with Jesus no matter what's going on around him or in him, is a must read for right now. This book will bless you and inspire you to move forward with Jesus too.
—David Norris, Lead Pastor City Church For All Nations in Bloomington, IN

As a builder of character, it refreshes me to know that Vad Lee is in the trenches to lead this next generation. Vad is a leader and understands his life is not defined by his titles and circumstances. As you read, you will witness Vad's passions on full display: His love for God, his love for his family, his love for people, love for the game of football, and a sense of humor are all-encompassing. This book will challenge you to go beyond the temptations of using status as a belief that you are walking in your true *purpose*. It will uplift and encourage you to peel back the layers of your heart to find your true *purpose*!
—Johnny Shelton, Baltimore Ravens Team Chaplain

Vad Lee is a God-loving and God-fearing man who has a passion for people and their relationship with Christ. In *Purpose over Position*, you will find his authenticity refreshing and powerful. He does a fantastic job of unpacking the lessons he's learned throughout his football career to guide us in living within God's divine will for our lives. There is power to be found in understanding the situations God leads us through, and Vad helps expand our Christian viewpoint as we move through seasons in our lives.
—Drew Mehringer, Florida Atlantic University Co-Offensive Coordinator, former Offensive Coordinator and Quarterbacks Coach at James Madison University

PURPOSE

over

position

Discerning God's Plan to Live a Life Full of Purpose!

VAD LEE

Carpenter's Son Publishing

Purpose Over Position

Published by Carpenter's Son Publishing, Franklin, TN.

Edited by Lee Titus Elliott

Cover and Interior Design by Adept Content Solutions

Printed in the United States of America

ISBN: 978-1-952025-22-8

CONTENTS

DEDICATION

To the person who loves God and needs greater understanding of purpose, this book is dedicated to you!

ACKNOWLEDGMENTS

To my wife, Khayla, thank you for exposing me to a new level of love and appreciation outside of what I do, and for loving me for who I am and becoming. Your patience and kindness is a great blessing for my growth as a man of God, a husband, and a father. I am so blessed that you have embraced this POP journey right by my side.

To my daughters, Saraiah and Sinaiah, I just want to make you proud and to create a strong foundation that will carry you through life. This book is a part of the legacy that I leave behind for you to cherish.

To all of my family and friends, you are loved and appreciated.

FOREWORD

I first met Vad Lee via a phone conversation two years ago when he was serving as FCA chaplain for Indiana University's Football program. Just by speaking with him, I knew right away that this young man was beyond his age in wisdom and maturity. One thing he made clear to me was that he wanted to fulfill the *purpose* that God has set for him, and that immediately drew me to him! You see, *purpose* to me is not just a word, it's *who we are* and *why we were created*. Living a life of purpose is simply a lifestyle led by our Lord and Savior, Jesus Christ! One of the reasons that I breathe is to summon other individuals to discover their life's purpose. The book you hold in your hands is written to do just that. Vad wrote this book with the purpose of building up leaders to understand the importance of living lives of *purpose over position*!

As a builder of men, it refreshes me to know that Vad Lee is in the trenches, fighting to lead this next generation. Vad is a leader, and he understands his life is not defined by his titles or his circumstances. As you read his words, you will witness Vad's passion on full display ; his love for God, his love for his family, his love for people, his love for the game of football, and his sense of humor are all-encompassing. This book will challenge you to go beyond the temptation of using status to support your belief that you are walking in your true purpose. It will uplift you and encourage you to peel back the layers of your heart to find your *true purpose*!

In closing, I'd like to share one of my favorite Scriptures and a favorite quote as they relate to living a life of purpose:

Lord, remind me how brief my time on earth will be.

Remind me that my days are numbered—

how fleeting my life is.

You have made my life no longer than the width of my hand.

My entire lifetime is just a moment to you;

at best, each of us is but a breath.

(Psalm 39:4–5 NLT)

"No individual has any right to come into this world and go out of it without leaving behind his/her distinct and legitimate reasons for having passed through it"

—George Washington Carver

It is my sincere prayer that you will read this book with your heart postured on realizing God's purpose for your life so that day by day, your position becomes secondary to your *purpose*!

Be Blessed, and I will talk to you soon

Till the *whole* world knows.

Johnny Shelton, Team Chaplain
Baltimore Ravens

INTRODUCTION

The inspiration for this book came after a devastating injury that I had suffered while playing NCAA Division I college football. As the quarterback for the Georgia Tech Yellow Jackets and James Madison Dukes, I found that life could not have been better. I was a two-time All-American and the conference Player of the Year, I also received national media attention: ESPN "Big Man on Campus," and a *Sports Illustrated* feature. My team was undefeated and was well on its way to a National Championship. But God had a different plan, and He allowed my life to take a turn. A record-breaking career was cut short and came to an end because of an injury sustained to my left foot. It wasn't until later that I begin to piece together God's marvelous purpose for my life. I spent years in uncertainty until one day I received a word from Him that would change my life forever. At this point, *Purpose over Position* was birthed, and this message is imperative for those who are striving to find meaning in their life's journey. I believe He will speak to the stay-at-home mother, the person with a dream, the business man who works long hours, the athlete on all levels, and the lukewarm community that needs that fire from the Lord. God has a special purpose for His creation. I pray that you will commit with me on this journey to discover all that God has for humanity through the lens of Scripture.

Purpose over Position (POP) is a motto that's been significant to me with its ability to transcend a person's life for a greater tomorrow. This book is comprised of inspirational stories and wisdom to help build up leaders toward a better future with hope. Oftentimes in life, we find ourselves stuck in positions that we may or may not like. On the job, we hope to climb the corporate ladder to the next promotion. On the sports team, we are competing to earn the starting spot. Within our everyday lives, we strive to become financially secure or gain a position that could potentially afford us the opportunity to accomplish more. Our position in life is always at the forefront of our minds because no one wants to be in a bad spot .

Early in my marriage, I wanted to be in a position to spoil my wife with gifts, buy a nice home to live in, and provide for my family in ways beyond their dreams! While those are, still my goals, early on it was far from our reality. As I learn more and more about my purpose, I no longer look to positional thinking; instead, I focus on my *purpose over position* to realize that everything in life has a meaning and contributes toward a greater future. My reason for writing this book is to help others discover their true purpose in life by not being defined by the weight of their titles or circumstances. I myself have experienced what it is like to live in divine purpose but also what it is like to live outside of it. It is important that all men and women understand their purpose in life.

A life that is not lived in purpose is a threat to our society, and it creates a foothold in the door for the enemy to toy with our minds. Your purpose is not based on your past circumstances or even what you may be going through now but is connected to your daily walk with God. Your purpose is bigger than the abuse you've once experienced; it's bigger than the job you were laid off from; it's even bigger than any relationship; it's also bigger than any setback you went through. Your purpose is in the hands of the Almighty God who has given us dominion in this world because He cares deeply for humanity. In this book, we will discuss what purpose is, and we will give examples of stories that will help reveal God's plan to live a life full of purpose. We will also refer to the Scriptures to gain a better picture of who God is and the purpose that He has destined for each of our lives.

CHAPTER 1

PURPOSE OVER POSITION

October 2015

It was a night filled with so much joy and anticipation, a night of good news, much more than I could have ever imagined. It was a night filled with so much fun, but it ended in so much despair —a night that I could never imagine or ever thought to even prepare for. It was the night when James Madison University, ranked number two nationally, would square off against its fierce rival, the Richmond Spiders, that were ranked number eleven nationally. The atmosphere in Bridgeforth Stadium was electric. Earlier that morning, *College GameDay* decided to broadcast its show live on the beautiful lawn of the James Madison campus. Students, fans, and the entire Harrisonburg community camped outside and flooded the scene to be a part of this historic moment. After all, the entire sports world was able to watch, on television, the perks of the James Madison College experience. ESPN analyst, Desmond Howard, went on record to tell the world that James Madison was the best environment ESPN had ever hosted its Saturday show, *College GameDay*. Howard's compliment could have come by surprise because *College GameDay* has hosted its show at major colleges and universities. However, for the compliment of those who have been a part of the James Madison University community, that was a normal environment in Harrisonburg, Virginia.

Playing in a sold-out stadium is what you dream of when you sign up to play college football. As expected, tens of thousands of fans were treated to an electrifying performance. I was playing my best football that night, and I had a really good feeling about defending our undefeated record against this very talented team. The rivalry lived up to the hype, as we exchanged a few touchdowns early in the game. After the two teams swapped leads several times, the score was tied up 28–28 at halftime. Our team prided itself at playing our best ball in the second half because we truly felt we were the stronger and better-conditioned team. So the second half that Saturday was ours to claim. However, we would be faced with a major bump in the road and one that I personally would have to endure.

It was second down, about the 37-yard line, on the left hash, momentum in our favor, and the ball was in my hands. Good things seemed to happen that night when the ball was in my hands. But on this particular play, I got tangled up on the left side when a Richmond defender grabbed my foot from behind. The momentum of my weight falling forward and the defender pulling my foot in the opposite direction caused ligaments in my left foot to tear apart. Little did I know, this one play would delimit my entire football playing career and be the cause of this being my last time putting on a James Madison uniform. I imagined when an athlete gets seriously injured, it would be a more graphic and gruesome scene. Though I do not wish injury upon myself or any athlete, the play that wrecked my football career would rank somewhere at the bottom in terms of impact. But, somehow, the pain of an awkward twist to my foot stood out above the rest.

As I took a second to get up, I remember thinking to myself, *It's just an ankle sprain, no big deal. I'll just walk it off*. Determined not to come off the field, I kept hobbling down the field for about five more plays, applying pressure on my only healthy foot, managing the offense in the running game and throwing the ball while off my back foot, which is a cardinal sin in the fundamentals of "quarterbacking." The pain never left like I thought it would; in fact, it only intensified, but I was strong-willed and determined to endure and finish. As we drove the ball inside our opponents' 15-yard line, our team was now faced with fourth down with two yards to go. Normally, it is no question who carries the ball in this situation, and it didn't even matter that our opponents knew this, too, because the quarterback power up the middle was our most effective play in this short-yardage situation. But because I had only one good foot, my coach decided to think the play over by calling a time-out.

Up until this point, I had been playing on pure adrenaline alone, but once the time-out was called, I had no other choice but to hobble over to the sideline and address my discomfort. While the coaches made necessary coaching adjustments, the medical staff attended to my foot. From the look on their faces, I knew this was not good. They quickly wrapped up my foot with more tape; I was sure that would do the trick, but when I applied pressure on it, I fell straight to my knees in the most pain that I've ever felt. Now the reality of not going back into the game began to clash with my emotions, as tears ran down my face. Before I could soak in the thought, I jerked away from the doctors, hobbled back over to my team for the play call. It was indeed our favorite short-yardage play, "Trey Right Up, 98 QB Blast." My heart sank, because I knew exactly what that might mean for my football future.

A true competitor never wants to come out of the game whether it's going in your favor or not, but it is important to discern what's best for the team. The thought of me being in the game would actually hurt my team, rather than help it, absolutely crushed my pride. I tapped my teammate and good friend Bryan Schor on the helmet, as a sign of support as he took over, while the medical staff escorted me to the locker room for x-rays. By the way, Bryan ignited the entire stadium as his quarterback power up the middle resulted in his trucking two Richmond defenders to gain the first down. Though it was difficult for me to show any happy emotions outwardly on my heart-rending walk to the locker, that made me so proud internally.

On my walk back into the locker room to get a X-ray, I remember looking back to the field of play. The reality of the referee blowing his whistle to start play but no longer being the guy out there taking the snap began to weigh heavily on my spirit. In this moment, I learned that sometimes life seems unfair and that you will be dealt with many obstacles along the way, but it is the way you respond to them that truly exemplifies your true character. As I tried to hold it together, I took what would be my final glimpse of the field in a college uniform. I noted that my coaches kept passionately coaching, that my teammates continued to play their hearts out, and that the fans kept on cheering loud and proud like they normally do. Life does not wait on anyone ; it continues to go on with or without you, no matter how you may feel about it .

Though I felt as if my world had come to an abrupt pause, the game of life surely carried on. I quickly discovered that positions in life are short-lived, but purpose lives forever. This is where my personal *purpose over position* journey began. Perhaps for you, it was losing a job, suffering an illness, a cancer diagnosis, a divorce in marriage, not passing the big test, or the challenges of living amidst a world pandemic. In the world we live in, we are all faced with different events that could alter our positions. Through this book, we will discover the depths of God's purpose over man's position and God's overall message of purpose. My prayer is that you will discover greater joy in your daily walk with God to live a life full of purpose beyond where you are today. The areas in your life that were once cloudy will become crystal clear, and the voice of God that you've been longing to hear will speak directly into your heart.

Discovery

Discovering your purpose may take minutes, hours, days, or years to fully embrace. Despite popular opinions from the bully at school or the egotistic person in the workplace or from the unsupportive family member or better yet, the world, God created you *on purpose*, *with purpose*, and *for purpose*. I hope you know this to be true, but even if you need an extra boost, you do have a special purpose that the world needs for you to discover. The way you see your purpose can determine the way that you view God. Persons who think that their purpose in life is too small spell "God" with a lowercase "g" instead of capital "G." Your God-given purpose should dictate your level of faith in God. It will be extremely difficult to operate in God's kingdom if you think that your life has little to no value. If this captures your viewpoint, then you must start with imposing truth to the enemy's lies. You are created with a unique purpose, which is designed specifically for you.

You have a special purpose that the world is relying on —a God-breathed purpose that is a kingdom solution to many earthly problems. Even when you are unsure or question your purpose, just keep on pressing forward. Famous NFL coach John Madden would say, " Don't worry about the horse being blind, just load the wagon." This is one of my favorite quotes of all time as it relates to purpose. Sometimes we may not always see or have a big-enough vision to know where we are going, but if we just keep plugging away by faith, putting in the necessary work, God will continue to lead us down the righteous path. When God is leading the charge, then all of our efforts will be purposeful toward a life of advancement, even when we cannot see what is ahead.

There are approximately 7.3 billion people in the world today. But the sad reality is that the majority of Earth's population will go unfulfilled or unaccomplished without discovering their purpose. Here's a list of suggested reasons why most end up not walking in purpose:

Fear of failure. Let's just be honest, experiencing failure in something that you are passionate about absolutely sucks! Whether it is a game, a test, or a relationship, it's important that you do not allow the fear of failure to hinder you from pressing on in life. Of course, it's in our nature to protect our feelings from any disappointments or setbacks. If an athlete could foresee an injury, he or she would most likely request to sit out that particular play. If Dr. Martin Luther King Jr. allowed death threats to stop him from creating change in the civil rights movement, we may have never experienced progress in equality for African Americans and all people today, though our fight continues. If you live life anticipating failure, you become mentally paralyzed and unable to move forward in purpose. Failure is not the opposite of success; it's part of the developing process in success that we must redefine. We will discuss this further in chapter four.

Procrastination or Laziness. Most people in life start off the journey toward purpose with great tenacity and effort. But as the days go by and life adds on more demands, the level of procrastination increases dramatically. This is what happens every year for many New Year's resolutions. Over 80 percent of New Year's resolutions fail to go past February. For example, to start off every year, gym memberships increase, financial savings increase, and libraries are packed with eager folks who vowed to read more books that year. Every day, we must build up the endurance to overcome procrastination and laziness. Famous poet William Ernest Henley wrote in his poem, "Invictus ": "I am the master of my fate, I am the captain of my soul." We determine if we will become masters of living out our divine purpose or become victims of laziness. We must be intentional in not allowing the sinking sand of procrastination to hinder us from progressing in purpose.

The Wrong Will. You can have the right intentions and the right motives but still not be in the will of God for Him to respond, act, or move. When we seek first the kingdom of God, the Holy Spirit begins to download His will to triumph over our own desires. This is a daily cleansing process that is even mentioned in Jesus's prayer in the Garden of Gethsemane, to realign His will to God's will. *"Father, if you are willing, please take this cup of suffering away from me. Yet I want your will to be done, not mine"* (Luke 22:42 NLT). Another passage of Scriptures is John 6:38 (NIV), *"For I have come down from Heaven not to do my will but the will of Him who sent me."* Those who have developed a strong will to attain purpose, no matter the cost, are pleasing to God. Lacking in willingness will only get you to the same spot tomorrow that you were in today. Willpower comes from a core conviction, where you won't settle for anything less than doing the will of the Father.

Discouragement. Have you ever heard these words before? "You are not good enough to do that." "That's a waste of time." I'm sure a friend, family member, or someone in a leadership position have states something similar to us . I have had experiences where a coach, family member, and/or friend tells me that I am not capable of something that was important to my life. In my younger days, I would use that as motivation to prove the naysayer wrong. However, even though that could serve as great motivation, on the flip side, holding on to negativity can be very exhausting and can rob you of God's joy.

> *Have I not commanded you? Be strong and of good courage; do not be afraid, nor be dismayed, for the LORD your God is with you wherever you go (Josh. 1:9 NKJV).*

Be of good courage, and he shall strengthen your heart, all ye that hope in the Lord (Ps. 31:24 KJB).

Have you ever shared a vision with a loved one but didn't get the response that you were anticipating? Such behavior is like getting punched in the gut by Mike Tyson (although I wouldn't wish that one upon anyone). Criticism that is not constructive or not supportive can cause many to become mentally paralyzed and thus discouraged from pursuing their vision. Do not let discouragement stop you from pressing forward! Not everyone can understand the burning desire and passion that you have inside of you. For most, only a select few will support your dream, passion, desire, or purpose equal to your desire, so be prepared to face objections but also be prepared to be of good courage. Don't let these objections stop your pursuit. Accept the challenge to live on purpose, despite the push back from others.

Pressure to Know. It is great to be ambitious, work hard, and plan for the future; however, most people don't have a clue what lies ahead. A question that all recent college graduates get almost immediately after walking across the stage is, "So, what are you going to do now?" I have personally refrained from asking young people that question because of the amount of pressure it adds. I absolutely hated answering that question when I was a recent graduate, trying to find my way. It felt embarrassing not being able to give a solid answer regarding my future endeavors. I have learned that life is going to throw many things at you, regardless of your plan. I want to encourage you that you do not need to know exactly what lies ahead ; all you need is trust in the Lord. Proverbs 3:5–6 (NIV) say that we should *Trust in the Lord with all your heart and lean not on your, in all your ways submit to him, and he will make your paths straight."* We do not need to know what lies ahead ; however, we need to know that God, our Father, has a purpose and a plan for those that trust His direction.

Little Faith. Trying to discover purpose outside of God is impossible. God is the brains behind one's purpose and one's operation. No thought or idea can go past Him, either in the flesh or in the spirit. Even Peter, a man who followed the ministry of Jesus for three years and who was one of the first disciples of the gospel, was a man of little faith when faced with a challenging feat of walking on water in the midst of a storm. However, Peter's training was a necessary lesson for all of us to learn so that even when we lack in faith, we can train ourselves to look past our position and focus on the position of Jesus to advance our faith.

God Honors Purpose

God honors our kingdom purpose within our earthly positions in life. In 1 Corinthians 10:31 (NLT), we read : "*Whatever you do, do it all for the glory of God.*"The key word in this passage is "whatever."The powerful thing about God is that He gives us the power of choice , a choice to do whatever we want : to sing, to dance, or to play. For the most part, we have a pretty good idea about things that are pleasing to God, and we also know the things that are not so glorifying to Him. However, sometimes we do not always make wise choices or at least choices that glorify the Father. We all have the choice to live a life full of purpose or live a life full of regret. Take Satan, for example, who wanted to be in God's position, so he began by worshipping himself, and, as a result of his disobedience, he and one-third of the angels that decided to follow him were cursed and removed from heaven, according to the Bible. Self-worship is clearly something that was not pleasing to the Father.

While purpose may be difficult to articulate in words, it must first align with God's Word.Your purpose is meant to draw you and others back to God. For example, if I shared with you two purpose statements of mine, which one would you consider to align more with God?

Purpose 1: My purpose in life is to play professional sports, make a lot of money, live comfortably, go to church, and to create a name for myself.

Purpose 2: My purpose in life is to serve the community, administer the gospel, and to empower less-fortunate families of the youth by building a homeless shelter.

In my humble opinion, I believe that God would honor Purpose Statement 2 because that purpose aligns directly with the Scripture. The focus is spreading the gospel, as Jesus commissioned the disciples to do in Matthew 28:18–20. Purpose Statement 2 also commits to tending to those who are less fortunate in the community —caring enough to establish a homeless shelter. Imagine more people supporting our youth, more people sharing the gospel, and more people empowering their community with labors of love. In return, I'm sure that more lives would be drawn to God's kingdom. The intentionality of serving will also build up one's faith .

Purpose Statement 1, on the other hand, has a great vision, but the priorities seem to focus on a singular position, status, money, and self-image, rather than glorifying the Father. And don't get me wrong, purpose statement 1 has some great goals in life, like playing a professional sport and making money , but we must ask ourselves, is this to build up God's eternal kingdom or man's earthly kingdom? In addition, "going to church" may sound like the right thing to say, but we must internally have a burning desire to grow in the Lord, or else going to church can turn into a weekly religious gathering that never penetrates the heart of action. What if I added to the purpose statement 1 "sharing Jesus with others"? Would this be more in alignment? Absolutely, because our purpose should draw us back to God and share the love of Jesus with all.

Before Jesus began His public ministry, he was moved by the Holy Spirit to fast in the wilderness for forty days and forty nights. There, he would be tried, tested, and tempted by Satan's best efforts to distract Him from His mission of purpose on Earth. Each time that Satan showed up, Jesus only responded with the Word of God, "It is written." In this, Jesus proves that his purpose statement is in direct partnership with the Word of God to be fulfilled. What if Satan came to try, test, and tempt you in the wilderness today? For many believers, that could be a very terrifying thought. But for those who indulge in the Word of God, both day and night, see the enemy as no competition because our purpose is connected to the eternal Word of God. The key to unlocking purpose is the Word of God! The only way we live a life full of purpose is when we embrace our kingdom purpose. I once heard a wise man say, "You can't teach a drowning man how to swim." This is a great visual for why it is a necessity to have a solid foundation in God's Word before being tested, tried, and tempted. We must immerse ourselves in the Word of God before we enter the test or else we will drown.

Being confident in purpose is an essential part of growing spiritually, psychologically, and emotionally. Although both purpose statements were able to be communicated in words, there should be a sole level of focus on advancing the Kingdom of God through His Word, rather than just advancing a personal agenda. As a reminder, whatever our hands find to do, we ought to do it all for the glory of God. We can be so focused on doing good things but yet still miss the mark of doing God things. When our life efforts align with His divine will, we get to experience life full of purpose despite our positions.

Before you go any further, I challenge you to take a second to reflect and to invite God into your space. Let this be an intimate moment between just you and God to reveal His purpose for your life. I urge you not to skip this instruction but instead to think deeply about what God wants from your life and to pray for clarity and direction in ways to become more mature in your daily pursuits of POP. I pray that you will discern God and that God will refine His promises to you. Once you are done reflecting, ask yourself this question: "Does my purpose statement align with the Word of God, or does it come from my own ambitions?" And if you have never written out a purpose statement, I encourage you to use this time to do so. Feel free to write it down in the margin of this page.

The Purpose of an Object

In 1869, Walter Camp, known historically as the "Father of American Football," implemented the first football game, with Princeton University facing off against Rutgers University. It has now been over 150 years since football fans experienced the first great game of American football. The game has become so popular in America that we fans have given it the title "America's Game." I'm sure Walter Camp would be proud of his contributions to the world of sports that has now become such an iconic part of our culture.

Let's take a look at how the actual football is used for play. Before we determine the purpose of this object, let's say you go to a gym with some buddies to play basketball. The only problem is there is no basketball in sight; instead, you see a football on the court. So you decide to substitute the oval-shaped ball for the missing basketball. How would this work? Would you still be able to play basketball the way it was intended? If you are anything like me, then you would do whatever just to have the opportunity to compete. For others, you are probably thinking this is a terrible idea. Playing basketball with a football is an object that is just not going to work. But let's dive a little deeper: why exactly would this object be a bad substitute for a basketball? After all, it is a ball, right?

Well, in order to answer that question accurately, we must first learn that, in 1934, Hugh "Shorty" Ray, a college football official at the time, is usually accredited with conceiving the pointed football that is used by teams today. The dynamics of the football have many elements that Shorty Ray designed exclusively for the intent of running, throwing, catching, and kicking—ultimately to score points or to defend against the opposing team from scoring. Its pointy tip is definitely not made to bounce on the hardwood floor but is perfectly designed to roll around on the grass (or turf) field. The football is not intended for shooting three-pointers, like Steph Curry, but rather for throwing touchdown passes, like your favorite quarterback (hopefully it's me, just kidding but serious). The basketball hoop was not designed for an oval-shaped object, but is more fitting for a round ball. Although it is indeed possible for a football to fit in the hoop, it is out of purpose, and we end up with a less enjoyable playing experience. Let's face it: we can never have success out of alignment, design, or purpose.

In life, sometimes we find ourselves using a football to shoot through the basketball hoop. Although playing basketball is not what the football was made for, we still try to land our shot in the basket anyway. It is similar to trying to put a round marble into a square hole—never a satisfying or successful result. We come to the understanding that the true purpose of anything lies with the intention of its creator. In our previous example, Camp, and later with Ray's additions , set the game of football apart for a specific purpose, intention, and design. In the same way, God the Father created us with a specific alignment, design, and purpose. He didn't create us in the wrong court or in the wrong field; rather, He created us as representation of His kingdom's purpose in our earthly positions. Living in purpose allows us to be aligned in the proper order to live life exactly how God intends for humanity. Therefore, you utilize the football on the football field and the basketball on the basketball court in its proper functions. Though you can actually play basketball with a football, I'm sure you would much rather live your life in total alignment, design, and purpose.

Chosen

While I was growing up, my favorite superhero, by far, was Spider-Man. What I love most about Spider-Man is that his story is relatable to the common person; just an ordinary kid, on an ordinary day, just so happened to get bitten by a not-so-ordinary spider. Have you ever been bitten by a spider? Unfortunately, I know the pain of being bitten by a spider, but, sadly I didn't turn into Spider-Man. In Peter Parker's story, that one spider bite changed the trajectory of his entire character. He went from being this average kid to a remarkable superhero. It took a process for him to learn how to utilize his newly found skill sets before there was even a thought of defeating bad guys. Before being bitten by the spider, he didn't ask to be a superhero or to have superpowers, but he was chosen as Spider-Man. Even without superpowers, we all have certain skill sets that we must embrace before we can fully utilize them toward our purpose. As we receive the beauty of life and the joy of purpose, we, too, can be superheroes like Spider-Man in our designated fields of power.

Purpose is not chosen by man; rather, it is chosen by God. When one receives that level of spiritual intelligence, it will change an entire perspective and even one's life. You can never be rejected when you have already been chosen. No matter how long it takes to come to fruition or how many times you have to take the test, you have been chosen. You are needed in places and in positions that you may not yet know, in order to fulfill God's calling for your life. When Peter Parker became Spider-Man, he embraced his calling. Embracing all of who God created us to be helps us to experience God's fruitfulness. No longer conforming to the ordinary; rather, with every breath, we become extraordinary in our field of purpose. You have been chosen by God to put on the mask of purpose and not humanity's position. It's up to you to receive that reward. When you are connected to the kingdom of God, you will automatically walk confidently as His chosen one. I find it interesting that Spider-Man could not fly on his own ability, but he had to use his spiderweb to elevate himself to different heights. We may not have spiderwebs, or superpowers, but we have the necessary gifts that will propel us to new levels of exuberance. According to Isaiah 40:31 (CBS), "*Those who trust in the LORD will renew their strength; they will soar on wings like eagles, they will run and not become weary, they will walk and not be faint.*"

God has given us the unique ability to soar over our positions in life by giving us dominion on Earth. In order to soar, we must operate in the skills that He has graciously outlined in the Scripture to humanity.

Trust—The word *trust* means depending on God for us to gain access to His ability to soar. In reality, God has generously created us with divine purpose to benefit our position. Our position does not define how high we soar. We must value and own trust as a necessary skill set that will advance our lives to reach new heights and new territory for the gospel's sake. Trusting may not always be easy, but it is always necessary for growth in relationships. In order to soar, we must first develop a trust relationship with God.

Strength—God has equipped us with His strength to overcome hardships. In the weight room, strength increases when a person continually challenges the muscles to deal with higher levels of resistance or weight. The more a person endures, the stronger he or she will become. In the supernatural, strength is available to the believer through abiding in His kingdom. Without God and the right perspective, it is impossible for one to renew his or her strength without resistance. The resistance that we endure in our daily pursuits can be for our benefit in the end. In order to soar, we must inherit the spiritual strength that is necessary to operate in a greater dimension.

Running—Always remember that life is a marathon and not a sprint. A marathon is long-lasting, while a sprint can last just seconds. One's purpose in life should be most interested in God's long-term glory, rather than one's temporary pleasure or emotion. It's important to keep steady by running your own race. In track, it takes a special focus because not only do you have to run , but you also have to stay in your own lane for most events. Crossing over into another lane would result in an automatic disqualification. Therefore, we ought to have a level of focus in running our own race. Running also builds up an endurance so that you can withstand the wind of opposition as you soar in life.

Walking—David, as a Psalmist, had the heart of a warrior. His words align with the dominion that God created in humanity: "*Even though I walk through the valley of the shadow of death, I will fear no evil, for you are with me; your rod and your staff, they comfort me*" (Ps. 23:4 ESV). How can a man in a world full of hatred and wickedness be so bold in the valley of death? He can be bold because he is assured that the Lord is with him and the Lord will protect him from his enemies. In other words, David is saying that he is not the one fighting the battles, but that it is the Lord's battle to win. Even the threat of an enemy's shadow cannot have rulership over our minds, emotions, and faith in the Lord. When a person is walking in a dark, deadly valley, the typical response would be to panic and run. However, I believe that David was speaking out loud to address his fears and to position himself in place of soaring above any doubt.

Soaring—Every person has the choice to operate in his or her kingdom purpose, even before reaching heaven. Living for eternity with kingdom purpose will allow man and woman to be empowered within their earthly position. It would be wise for men and women to see life from the lens of the kingdom vantage point. When people have trouble seeing, their only options are either to get prescription glasses or contact lenses. Likewise, when we are desperate to look beyond our circumstances, the only option is to tap into the spiritual realms. What is the point of being created by a powerful God if His creation is powerless? We ought to earn our wings to fly and to see life from God's perspective. Some of the challenges that we face in life may not appear as big as we perceive them to be with the right perspective. But you must have a kingdom perspective to overcome life's challenges and must shift into a position of soaring with the Lord Almighty.

Author's Motivation:
Eliminate to Elevate

As a quarterback trainer, one of the many ways that I reach my athletes is by reminding them of their skill, technique, and development. We use the phrase "Eliminate to Elevate." This phrase highlights our pursuit to eliminate bad habits, such as false stepping, improper mechanics, and throwing angles in order to elevate to a greater performance. In order for us to elevate, the elimination process is a very critical element toward the goal. In the same way, as we strive to live a purposeful lifestyle, we must eliminate areas in our lives that hinder us from elevating. Elevation is like a staircase; you start from the bottom, and you have to work yourself up to the top. Each step takes focus and determination, as there is a natural rhythm of your steps.

It's important we find our supernatural rhythm of focus on each step of purpose so we do not trip up and fall flat on our faces. In order to attract purpose, we must elevate our unique skills, talents, and thoughts, and use the wisdom God has given us to reach the next step. It takes focus and determination to keep going because sometimes we don't quite know where the staircase ends. You can be at the bottom of the staircase today, but elevation is only one step away. When you elevate, you eliminate fear, failure, and insecurities from your mind. Keep going; don't stop. It is time to elevate our faith journey to another level.

CHAPTER 2

WHO ARE YOU?

The Beginning

Who are you? In order to spread your wings and to have a clear understanding of your purpose in life, you must understand who you are! And, in order to understand who you are, you must first understand who God is! And, in order to understand who God is, it's important to study our life manual: the Bible. The Word of God is indeed the greatest resource for humanity to live a life full of purpose.

> *So God created mankind in his own image, in the image of God he created them, male and female he created them.* (Genesis 1:27 NIV)

Genesis, the first book of the Bible, shares the genealogy of mankind's existence. God clearly made it known that He had created humanity in His likeness and in His image, *the imago Dei*. We ought to be captivated by this discovery about who we truly are. God is "The Lion of Judah," "the Alpha and the Omega," "the Truth and the Light," "the Omniscient," "the Lamb of Righteousness," "the Great I Am," and "the Great Shepherd," which are just a few names that embody who God is. Whoa, every person must pause and reflect—and not miss this incredibly good news! This truth leads us to determine that God cares so deeply about who you are that He was willing to shape you in His own image and glory. This piece of knowledge alone is a great blessing in discovering our kingdom identity as we live on Earth.

When I was young, I had a great deal of success as an athlete, particularly in football. I remember thinking, "Football is who I am; this is the purpose that God created me for." I was sure that playing football was my ultimate purpose in life, and I was sure that God made me for this very reason. Well, I wish my younger self would have meditated on Genesis 1:27; as it disproves my immature theory because God determines who we are by creating us in His likeness and image, not in the image of what we do. God is highly offended when we credit other things to compete with His original design of who we are and whose we are. A profession is not who we are; rather, it is only what we do. So no matter what job title you may carry today or how many benefits you may receive from it, remember that you were chosen as God's beloved son and daughter, whom He loves dearly.

Beloved

For a moment let's take a look at the historical account of Jesus's baptism in Mark chapter one.

> In those days Jesus came from Nazareth of Galilee and was baptized by John in the Jordan. Immediately coming up out of the water, he (John) saw the heavens torn open, and the Spirit like a dove descending on Him (Jesus); and a voice came out of heaven saying: "You are My beloved Son, in You I am well-pleased and delighted!" (Mark 1:9 AMP)

This is such good news! God the Father publicly honored Jesus as His beloved son to the entire world, and He was very happy to do so. *Beloved*, *well-pleased*, and *delighted* are a few empowering words that God used to describe Jesus. What I love most about this scene in Scripture is that this validation from the Father in heaven came before Jesus's ministry platform of healing the sick, opening the eyes of the blind, and resurrecting the dead from the grave. Before Jesus did any of these amazing signs and wonders that we read about, God was already delighted and well-pleased in His Son, Jesus. Jesus did not have to earn the Father's love by obtaining certain positions in life but only by living out His divine purpose.

As we read this truth about God's character, do we find it difficult to believe that we are the beloved sons and daughters of God and that He is well-pleased and delighted in us personally too? Maybe for most, that can be a very hard question to discern. Perhaps someone might even feel that this particular Scripture and scene in the Bible only applies to Jesus since He is the only sinless man to ever walk the earth as God in the flesh and purposed for the remission of sin. If you are one to think that, I would gracefully encourage you to reflect on whose image and likeness you obtain. God the Father, Jesus the Son, and the Holy Spirit live within, right? We should be confident that the Creator God is pleased with His creation in you. It should be encouraging and empowering to live our lives knowing that the Father is delighted and well-pleased because you are a reflection of Him and the product of His personal artwork.

Even before the job, the house, the spouse, the ministry, the fame, the game, the finances, and your wildest dreams, it's important that we understand that He is "well-pleased" when we align our lives in unity and community in Him. This means that we must delight in who we are as God's image bearers. With this revelation in mind, I can almost feel the weight of each reader being lifted off to no longer perform or chase after temporary, earthly things. No longer would we find ourselves trying to figure out how to get verified on our social media page or see how many likes we attract on Instagram—a pat on the back by our peers—but instead walk in purpose knowing that we are pleasing to the Father. Jesus was verified to the whole world the moment that He came out of the baptism water, before He had done any miracles or started His ministry. The closer we are to God, the more we hear His voice. The more we hear God's voice, the more we know where we stand. It's important to stay connected to Him daily so that we become empowered each and every day, pleasing the Father!

Elevate Your Position

We were chosen to be great. Our purpose provides the greatness that we long for in our worldly positions. It is not the position that gives us purpose but God's divine presence that is aligned with it. What divine position has God placed on your heart that in turn produces divine eternal impact? Although these positions do not make up who we are, they can play a part in shaping who we are to become and what we are to fulfill. In both success and in unsuccessful moments, we must remain under the umbrella of God's divine purpose over position .

Take for instance my wife, Khayla, who is a dental student at the historic Howard University studying to earn her Doctor of Dental Surgery degree. Khayla has a huge heart toward educating people on the importance of dental hygiene, especially in communities that lack in dental health resources. However, her journey of getting to dental school was a path of detours. Personally, I am grateful to have witnessed how hard Khayla has worked to make her dream become true. Her vision of becoming a dentist dates back to her youth. During her undergrad at Clark Atlanta University, God affirmed His purpose for Khayla to make a difference in the dentistry field by giving her the vision of "Ministry, Dentistry." No longer does Khayla consider this just as a dream, but it is her divine duty to serve God's people in a way that will be beneficial for their overall health.

At twenty-seven-years old, being five years removed from undergrad, married to yours truly, and a mother of two precious daughters (Saraiah and Sinaiah), this isn't exactly how Khayla envisioned her dental school journey to begin. In fact, Khayla was destined to begin her dental school career five years earlier, but after two low qualifying scores on her Dental Examination Test, she did not qualify for acceptance into a dental program. As you can imagine, Khayla has had to grapple with the agony of years going by with an unfulfilled dream, classmates passing her by, and the fear of missing out on her divine calling. Nevertheless, I love that the story does not end here because though we may face trials and tribulations along the way, God remains faithful to His beloved children, and He delights in making a way even when it seems like an impossible feat. Khayla did not give up, and this was just the beginning of her personal purpose over position testimony. Although we may not always get what we want at the time we want it, God's timing is greater than our own time! A person who never gives up does not end in failure but acquires necessary lessons and experiences that will ultimately benefit them in pursuit of their calling. This in turn sets up that person for a much greater outcome and testimony.

While Khayla had spent years as a stay-at-home mother, she gained valuable skill sets along the way that now benefit her "Ministry, Dentistry" calling. I personally believe that these three years have matured her to fully embrace the woman of God that she is outside of the admired white coat position but also taught her that "*God's Word will not return to me empty, but will accomplish what I desire and achieve the purpose for which I sent it*" (Isa. 55:11 NIV). Through the years of preparation, Khayla now understands what it's like to live with the assurance of first being God's beloved daughter in whom He is well-pleased and delighted in, even before becoming a doctor in dental medicine. How awesome is it when the time comes for Dr. Khayla Lee, the beloved daughter of God, a reflection of God's image and likeness, to treat her patients' teeth with greater assurance of God's word—"Ministry, Dentistry." There are millions of people who will one day yearn for her dental treatment services, and not only will their teeth be in better shape, but their spirits will encounter the favor of the Lord. It's extremely important that we are careful to not allow temporary things, such as jobs or degrees, to determine how much God loves and favors us. However, when the Holy Spirit speaks, we should listen; and when He moves, we should go. Khayla's passion for dentistry carries a much deeper conviction as she pursues to live out her kingdom calling with her dental career.

His Glory, Our Good

When God speaks, we should be quick to listen because it is for our good and His glory. I will never forget the day when my small-group leader, Kenny McFarland, encountered a homeless man during Victory Church ATL 's initiative to feed the homeless. This particular individual was searching for food and clothing in the dumpster. After Kenny offered him some food, the two began to have an open dialogue about life. Somewhere in the conversation, the homeless man felt led to share that his purpose in life is to inspire and encourage the youth. He had shared his story so eloquently that, at the time, I was puzzled, given his current conditions. Let's be honest, how many parents would sign up their kids for 101 with a man who lives on the streets and finds leftovers from the trash can? Probably not many. On the other hand, I could only imagine what this man's ministry could look like if he was in a better position in life. I could picture him well dressed, maybe on a stage with a microphone, speaking to hundreds or thousands of youth, inspiring and teaching them fundamental principles of faith in God.

As the man kept talking, he shared that although he would rather not be homeless while fulfilling his purpose, God was still using him as an instrument to share his testimony and to encourage people who walk by his path. His platform may not have been ideal, but God had graced him to still operate in greater purpose. Although he didn't foresee himself in that position, he was able to touch and relate to the people within his community. If there is no effort to minister outside of the church walls, then there is less opportunity to empower the community to receive the Good News. As a young man myself, I feel more empowered by how God can still use this poor man's position to glorify greater purpose. No matter what position you find yourself in today, God still has plans to prosper the purpose that He has assigned to your life. God will always get the glory, one way or another. If the homeless man can reach others in his situation, then it should be an encouragement that our purpose is greater than our position and that we can still live a life full of purpose. What God places inside of each and every person must manifest in our lives for our good and His ultimate glory.

Jonah

The book of Jonah shares insight on how God intervened in one man's rebellion. Jonah wanted to give up and go the opposite way of the Lord's instruction. This kind of disobedience led God to take action by sparing Jonah's life in the mouth of a whale. Can you imagine what his life was like inside the belly of a whale somewhere out in the middle of the sea —no internet connection, no cell phone service, no book to read, no sunlight, and no sense of direction

? I imagine that Jonah's diet probably consisted of leftover krill and salt water to drink during his three-day stay in the belly of a whale.

At that point, Jonah would have much rather died than to be saved and do what God instructed him to do. Can you imagine going into the worst community that you can think of to preach the gospel—gang related activates, gun violence, drug consumption, alcohol abuse, and just an overall bad environment? Your being new to the community would most likely get dealt with immediately. While Nineveh did not have these particular sets of issues, it was the most powerful and ruthless city in that day. God had sent Jonah on assignment to stir up revival to the lost and wicked souls of Nineveh. However, Jonah wanted nothing to do with this assignment and allowed fear to prevent him from pursuing purpose! God's way of disciplining Jonah was by positioning him in the belly of a whale to discover and discern who he was in Christ. It was during that time that Jonah had got the courage to carry God's message forward to Nineveh. Again, when God speaks, it is best for us to listen in obedience. God always will get the glory, one way or another. For insight, let's read Jonah 1:1–4, 7–8 (NLT):

> The Lord gave this message to Jonah son of Amittai:"Get up and go to the great city of Nineveh. Announce my judgment against it because I have seen how wicked its people are." But Jonah got up and went in the opposite direction to get away from the LORD. He went down to the port of Joppa, where he found a ship leaving for Tarshish. He brought a ticket and went on board, hoping to escape from the LORD by sailing to Tarshish. But the Lord hurled a powerful wind over the seas, causing a violent storm that threatened to break the ship apart . . . Then the crew cast lots to see which of them had offended the gods and caused the terrible storm. When they did this, the lots identified Jonah as the culprit. "Why has this awful storm come down on us? **Who are you?**"

The ship's crew asked Jonah the same question that we started this chapter with: "Who are you?" In order to have a clear understanding of your purpose in life, you must first understand who you are! And in order to understand who you are, you must understand who God is. God will use the unlikeliest ways to lure you back into purpose and in position with Him. He can use the position of a man living on the street or the position of a scary man in the belly of fish to advance the calling that He has given to us. You are no exception from God's plans manifesting to align with His will for your life. You do not need to be positioned in a trash can or the mouth of a whale to help make who you are in God intently. Instead, use these stories as motivation so we do not find ourselves in the midst of similar positions.

Author's Motivation: Press On

In the beginning of 2018, I participated in tradition with coming up with a word of the year. As I drew inspiration from God's Word, I came across a passage in Philippians 3:14 (NIV), "I press on toward the goal to win the prize for which God has called me heavenward in Christ Jesus." *As an athlete, this Scripture is loaded with athletic lingo that I could definitely relate to pretty well. The phrase* press on *has become one of my new favorite mottos of encouragement to others. Little did I know that 2018 would be one of the hardest years of my life, as my family and I had to endure many challenging situations. We lost our jobs, important friendships, and financial leverage that we had been accustomed to. Our family of four even had to move into a one-bedroom at my mother-in-law's place. As I spare you the details, I believe that year God allowed for us to experience what a press-on lifestyle consisted of and feels like.*

Pressing on is the matter of the will inside of you to embrace the deserted moments in our lives for the benefit of spiritual maturity. Anything you do in life will never come easy, and quite frankly, it shouldn't. God created us all in His image, meaning that we all have inherited the unique gifts, qualities, and skills of our Creator to subdue and cultivate the earth. Paul, the writer of Philippians, is a man who experienced a lot of hardships and persecution for spreading the gospel, but his motivation was to press on toward the goal to win his kingdom reward and not the earthly prize. In life, we must obtain intentionality toward everything that we pursue, no matter how tough or hard the situation may appear. We have to choose to press on in order to move forward. Even though pressing may come with some resistance, God is right there beside us, pushing us through.

CHAPTER 3

REDEFINE SUCCESS

A s a two-time All-American and team captain, I often reminisce on my college-football-playing days. My favorite memories are scoring touchdowns, being in the locker room with the guys, and beating up on our opponents. One memory I'll never forget was the historic night in Dallas, Texas, as the James Madison Dukes (JMU) took down Southern Methodist University (SMU) in 2015. That night, JMU made college football history by being added to a short list of FCS teams to beat an FBS opponent. We took the lead with only a few seconds left for the final score of 48–45. I made history of my own by breaking the all-time single-game passing and rushing performance record in college football history. I had no idea until the press conference afterward that I had run for a career high of 276 yards, passed for another 289 yards, and had scored four touchdowns. I was involved in over 500 yards of total offense that night.

This performance had solidified my legacy at JMU forever, and it solidified what I thought would be my chance as a future NFL star. As a result, days later, the major news outlet, ESPN, sent an entire film crew to follow me around JMU's campus to air its "Big Man on Campus" segment. My performance was featured in *Sports Illustrated* magazine, which is one of the leading sports magazines in the world with roughly over 2 million subscribers. In addition weeks later, *College GameDay*, the most popular college football television show, decided to host its *Saturday Morning Pre-Game* show on the lawn of JMU's quad square! What success looked like for me at that time was winning games, making decent grades, and living the college dream as the "Big Man on Campus."

My status as the starting quarterback brought national attention and campus popularity. I remember forgoing the questions of wise leaders when they would ask, "What do you plan to do outside of the game of football?" At that point of my life, I had a hard time with answering that question, because of my investment and identity as a player. I had given sports every ounce of energy, and the closer I got to what I perceived would be a successful career, the less vitality I had to give to other trades.

Steve Wilson, a retired NFL athlete, collegiate coach, and mentor to many, including me, is known for his many sayings that we have all grown fond of. He would often say, "The only thing that is guaranteed about the game of football is that one day you will become an ex-football player." Whether you played ten seasons or ten plays of a sport, the one thing that every athlete shares in common is one day no longer being able to play. I surely wish that I could have met and heard Coach Wilson say this early on in my journey. Perhaps, I would have taken my public policy classes a little more seriously at JMU or developed a greater passion for my business classes at Georgia Tech. But unfortunately my youthful thought process was that positions were meant to last. And maybe I wasn't so naïve to think that it would last forever but at least longer than my reality.

Growing up from the time when I was five-years old, all I ever knew was my love for the game, and I could not imagine life without it. We all have aspirations and certain passions, but let it be known that those things should not define who we are. The world is constantly trying to identify us with titles and positions. Even on the job, we walk around daily with a name tag or company's logo pinned to our shirts. Though it is great to be identified by a great brand or great organization, we should first yearn to be identified as a kingdom citizen of God (See Matt. 6:33). The kingdom helps us to set our eyes upon God's ultimate purpose over man's temporary position. To Coach Wilson's point, the only thing guaranteed about life positions is that one day, it will become your past position.

As we discern the beauty of life's positions, we must consistently redefine what success looks like for our lives. Successful leaders have the ability to properly discern the times to redefine, to enhance, and to meet the demand of life's current positions. This is so important for our personal overall growth and development. Most of us have developed our images of success from the wrong sources. Many of us have looked to Hollywood, entertainers, and politicians as the ideal image. But if you take a close look into the lives of these same people that the world idolizes, you will quickly find out that they too have experienced some unsuccessful moments, which have caused them to redefine their circumstances. In order to become an effective leader in our field of life, we must redefine success through the characteristics of leadership and through the lens of God. We must go back to God's promises, and we must lean on Him to direct us in the right way. God's purpose for our lives is much more important than previous self-image, celebrity status, job position, pay scale, and titles.

The Living Word

> *For the word of God is living and powerful, and sharper than any two edged sword, piercing even to the division of soul and spirit, and of joints and marrow, and is discerner of the thoughts and intents of the heart. (Heb. 4:12 NKJV)*

It took me three years to be able to watch a football game on TV once my career was uncertain after my last snap in the Canadian Football League (CFL). I no longer had the same passion, care, and joy that I once had my entire life since the age of five. Instead I felt a lot of anger, bitterness, and disappointment to say the least. After a while, I realized that this was bigger than me not being able to watch games on TV, but I was so emotionally unstable because this huge part of my life felt empty. I just could not fathom how I gave this game so much of my heart, love, and dedication just to end up broken in injury. I also couldn't understand how I could be *the first player in Division 1 history to run and pass for over 270 yards in one game*, and the NFL did not take notice. I couldn't understand how I was a two-time All-American and conference player of the year but still gained no real respect.

It just did not make any sense to me, how I'd been praised my whole life for my athletic ability, but now I am being told that I am not good enough, tall enough, and smart enough to play on the big stage. Finally, what blew my young mind was when I would see a person who was less talented and less statistically proven than me get a clear shot to compete in the NFL. There were many dark days as these type of thoughts would plague my mind, especially if I had given attention to the game. It took days, weeks, and years for me to truly embrace my position outside of sports. As I reflect back now, I can honestly say, God's sweet whispers of "purpose over position" and His living Word was the very thing that I could count on to get me through. Once I began to anchor my thoughts and emotions on His Word, I began to be delivered from my anger toward my football story. As I was so desperate for some good news in my life, God sent it through His divine and living Word.

Redefine

What does success look like for you? Have you ever written down the plan to achieve that success? Success can be based on circumstances, lifestyle, education, jobs, finances, relationship goals, and accomplishments. As you gain life experiences, success can very well alter or even change over time. Oftentimes, people lose confidence in their ability to obtain success because of the misperception of what success really is due to not being in the position that they've once desired. In life, we can find ourselves getting ahead of God. The mask of our fancy degrees, job titles, materialistic possessions, and dreams of what could be increases our independence to feel as though success is based on our efforts alone and not God's perfect will for our lives. However, we must run our race of life fully equipped with God's original design of success.

Success is ultimately what God says it is specifically for your life! Your life success is predicated on God's intentional purpose for you, which is a solution to an earthly problem. God's plans for success for one's life could be as simple as managing roles, such as an evangelist role, teacher role, carpenter role, financial supportive role, or caregiver role. We can assume many roles in this life, but a successful person assumes the role appointed by God for the greater good of His glory. It starts with a mind shift of redefining our vision of success, which can be limited to our earthly understandings of what appears to be a successful life. We must take a greater look at the word *redefine*, in order to discover its roots. According to *Online Etymology Dictionary*, the prefix *re* implies "to go back to the original place, again, anew, once more." The word *define* means "to specify; to fix or establish authoritatively." The power comes in when the prefix *re-* and the word *define* partner together, they imply that you should go back to the original meaning that God has already given specifically and authoritatively to your life. It is a shift of focusing on the divine spiritual manifestation of God that redefines the natural wisdom of man. With this knowledge, we can understand how to embrace a redefine lifestyle which implies anew, fresh, original, specific, and the anointing of kingdom success. It is simply reconceiving what is already yours in order to live a purposeful life.

Platform or Purpose

Many young people have big dreams and aspiration to become the next president, astronaut, firefighter, and other very important careers. For me, I dreamed of becoming the next great National Football League (NFL) quarterback, to win a few Superbowls, and to be considered as one of the all-time greats. Fortunately, my life did not play out as I had once imagined it would, and because of that, I have a much greater appreciation for God's plan. Because of my idolization of NFL players' success, I once assumed that the only way I could become successful in life was to be in their position. After all, their lives seemed to fit in the image of an American's view of what a successful and purposeful life was. I remember thinking that the only way for me to advance my family forward financially was to make millions in the NFL. The only way to create positive change and make a difference within my community was based on having this huge NFL platform. I was overwhelmed with the thought that I could only live a successful life by playing in the NFL. In my failure to achieve my dream, I was left with this simple question, "Am I pursuing God's purpose or the famous platform of a professional athlete?" Purpose or Platform is another POP acronym that I was reminded of in order to get over my own desire to focus on God's divine plans for my life. My thoughts and plans had to be redefined from idolizing platform to embracing God's purpose.

Can unfulfilled dreams teach us life lessons? Is there a lesson in suffering a loss? You bet there are, and praise God that there is so much more to life than one ideal image of success. I have met so many wonderful doctors, lawyers, artist, and entrepreneurs who have all had those redefining moments in their life journeys in order to reach the level of success that they are living in now. Discerning God's plan to live a life full of purpose will require one to redefine success in order to realign the flesh with the spirit of God's purpose for your life. Young people should pursue their dreams and goals but only with the viewpoint to please our Heavenly Father and be reminded that ultimately your purpose and identity are not defined by what you do, but who you are. You are a child of God, and He has prosperous plans for you. Having vision early on in life is very important for the fundamental development for young people because vision is a preview of your purpose to inherit.

However, we must be prepared to redefine success along the journey, so you will not deem your life as failure if life takes a turn in a different direction than you originally planned, even if that means your dreams are crushed. Personally, I believe that your visions, goals, and ideas of success will ultimately lead you to greater kingdom purpose, even without ever having to experience what the world would call success. Some of my goals have been a great success and some not so successful, but having goals has benefitted me entirely toward God. My advice is by no means intended to crush one's dreams, visions, or goals; rather, it is intended to highlight God's Word so that although he plans his ways, only the Lord will determine his steps. I once heard a great person of God say "plan like it depends on you, but pray like it depends on God." My advice is to plan in pencil; as you discern God's penned plans for your life, do not be afraid to ask God to direct your vision with His good and perfect will for your life. "*If you remain in me and my word remains in you, ask whatever you wish and it will be done for you*" (John 15:7 NIV). When we are aligned with God's will, He gives us the desires of our heart. It wasn't until later that I was able to piece together that God used football as a vehicle to advance my education, to gain new life experiences, to develop divine relationships, and to advance my vision of success.

PAUSE MOMENT: Take a moment to do some self-evaluation on your personal image of success.

Have your pencil prepared to write down the things that come to mind. Invite God into your space as you divinely plan according to His will and not your own. In what ways could you redefine success to give you the best perspective to move forward with God in mind? Maybe even think back to ten years ago and evaluate your ideas of a successful future. Where in your life story must you redefine your life's direction, according to God's will? Think through ways that you can best serve your athletic career, education, business endeavors, and faith toward greater kingdom purpose.

Redefining success not only allows you to let go of the weight of empty goals, but it also helps you to discern God's plans with total submission. God is wiser than your greatest image of achievement. God has made each individual person to become successful. He does not consider one particular career above another, and He has no favorite business endeavor over another. Society may place certain idolizations to specific careers, such as getting paid the big bucks to play ball on national television, but those careers that are aligned with kingdom purpose are a really big deal to God too. We should be very thankful that He has equipped us with the fundamental functions that are needed to live an abundant life .

We often overlook the very breath that we breathe. Humanity was lifeless until God blew breath into man's nostrils in the very beginning of creation (see Gen. 2:7). Otherwise, we would have just gone back to dust before He used the resource to form us. It is so powerful that this one breath from God continues to transpire life in humanity for thousands of years. Also, the fact that each part of the body functions for a specific purpose. Take for instance, your eyelashes, which prevent things from falling in your eyes; your nose hairs stop elements from flying up into your nostrils; even your nails protect the most sensitive parts of your bodies. Now, these functions may seem very minute details to highlight, but in turn these functions make a huge impact in our daily lives. All the minute details add up toward the embracing of understanding and redefining what success can look like.

Embrace Change

We cannot expect things, situations, and circumstances to always remain the same in our lives, including success. The world is constantly evolving in all phases of life. Therefore, we must embrace change because it is necessary for our physical and spiritual growth, along with psychological development. The reality is that only a small percentage of people actually respond to change appropriately and effectively. Change over time has been perceived as a bad thing, but it shouldn't be. Change, in fact, is inevitable. It takes a great mental shift for one's mind to first see change as something positive instead of negative. Change does not have to result in failure; rather, it can also be marked as a great success, with the proper care.

I remember challenging this thought process when my circumstances changed once I stopped playing football. After not making it onto an NFL roster, I felt cheated because my life was leading up to that moment I'd worked my entire life for, just to be let down and what most would considered to be failure. During that time of my life, I was so emotionally unstable. For the first time in my life, I had to face myself in the mirror without the extra titles of quarterback, football star, and All-American, but now I was only left with myself to face in the mirror. After giving my all to the daily grind of practices, early morning workouts, and offseason trainings, year in and year out, I was now left with figuring out life beyond my normal routine.

Change constantly happens to us, through us, and around us. We must be ready to grasp this understanding in order to move forward in a healthy manner. In his book, *The Principles and Benefits of Change*, Dr. Myles Munroe breaks down the importance of change as he describes change as being "weighed by its outcome: you make a decision that improves your life, or you make a choice that shatters your dreams. Change is measured in gains and losses: begin a career, or end a career; find a spouse, or lose a loved one; receive a promotion or lose a job."[1]

How we respond to change will ultimately determine if it will be a positive or a negative outcome in our life. During my and my teammates' offseason training in college football, one of our most beneficial drills was called the "Sudden Change Drill." Instead of our strength and performance coach giving us the promised thirty-second rest break in between our wind sprints, he would randomly yell out, "Sudden change" at any moment during the thirty-second recovery time. In our exhaustion, we all knew to quickly jump back

---

1   Munroe, Myles (2009). The Principles and Benefits of Change: Fulfilling Your Purpose in Unsettled Times. New Kensington, PA: Whitaker House.

on the line in the ready position to anticipate his whistle to begin our next sprint. I had a strong dislike for the sudden change drill, but looking back it was very beneficial for our teams preparedness. "Sudden change" is a drill to emulate a real-game scenario in practice so we would be prepared for an unexpected change of events in the actual game. Fumbles, interceptions, and turnovers happen all the time in the game of football, so it's important that you stay locked into the game, even when it may be your turn to take a sideline break. You never know when there will be a change of possession.

Our coach's intentions for these drills were to prepare our minds and our bodies to respond to change in a positive way. We never knew when these sudden-change moments would happen, but all throughout practice we could be assured that they would happen. If you are not prepared for changes in life, then situations will inevitably control you. Imagine being on the sideline of a football game, hanging out and not really paying attention to the game. A "sudden change" moment happens in the game, but you misplaced your helmet and can't find it. You would not be prepared for that change of events. This, in turn, is not beneficial for you or your team's success. On the flip side, when you are engaged and are actively prepared for things to change, then you can use change as a positive outcome in your life.

The night that Jesus was betrayed by Judas, Peter had a very difficult time accepting the change to come as a positive outcome. When Jesus made His disciples aware that one of them would betray him, Peter was ready to deal with that individual by being the first to ask Jesus, "Who?" Only a few verses later, Peter was rebuked by Jesus, cut off a high priest's ear by a sword, and denied Jesus three times in Luke, chapter 22, as a result of sudden change. What a rough stretch of events for Peter. His heart always seemed to be in the right place, but his responses were all wrong. Jesus wanted him to embrace the change that needed to happen in order to advance the gospel message forward. I believe that Jesus shared these things with Peter, not to condemn him, but to highlight the importance of sudden change in life. Although Peter was left with all this guilt in his heart, the real message behind Peter's actions was that they didn't come as a surprise to God; instead, He already had grace for Peter's shortcomings as He was preparing him for sudden change in life. Sudden change is a huge part of the process of redefining success. I'm sure Peter must have felt horrible in these moments, but because of God's grace for him, he was allowed to redefine his future success as one of the greatest disciples to walk with Jesus.

> For you know very well that the day of the Lord will come like a thief in the night. ³While people are saying, "Peace and safety," destruction will come on them suddenly, as labor pains on a pregnant woman, and they will not escape. ⁴But you, brothers and sisters, are not in darkness so that this day should surprise you like a thief. (1 Thess. 5: 2–4 NIV)

Are you preparing to stay, or are you preparing to leave? When you learn to adopt the kingdom's perspective, you no longer idolize living in the world but are equipped with heaven's agenda. Scripture clearly states that no one knows the hour or the day of the Lord Jesus Christ's return. Furthermore, it states that He *"will come like a thief in the night"* (1 Thess. 5:2) —meaning that it may not be a time that is convenient for you, but a time convenient for His master plan. However, believers should be discerning the times and should be prepared for His return. The reality is He can even come today. If He does, are you eternally prepared for the sudden change? He has graced you to live today so that you can be prepared for His return. Therefore, we must prepare ourselves through His marvelous Word, His holy assignments, and His divine direction. This world is not your home, and if you claim to be a follower of Jesus Christ, then you should be elated to reunite with Him in His eternal kingdom soon.

Examples of Change Embraced

A few worldly examples of success redefined: Thomas Edison invented the original lightbulb; however, Lewis Latimer created a newer lightbulb by using a carbon filament. Latimer's creation increased the life span of the original lightbulb from a few days to several months. Thomas Edison will always be a success story as the inventor of the original light bulb, but thank God for Lewis Latimer for having created an even longer-lasting lightbulb. This is success redefined!

Besides Lewis Latimer, Garrett Morgan also redefined success. Imagine driving down a road or a street, and the upcoming traffic light switches abruptly from green light to a red light. I can only imagine the disasters that would be created while driving in traffic in Washington, DC. Back in the early 1900s, there was only a two-light system, green meaning go and red meaning stop. However, after witnessing a horrific car crash at an intersection, Mr. Morgan decided to invent a "yield" component added to the center of the horizontal traffic light. This "yield" component is the yellow light that we are all so familiar with today, which warns oncoming drivers of an impending stop. Garrett Morgan, with his invention of the yellow light, helped enhance the safety of streets and saved millions of lives. Fulfilling purpose, even from a lightbulb, can change and impact an entire world. Did these men grow up with these as their ideas of purpose and success in life? Probably not, but these incredible inventions by these men have inspired greater life operations.

> *And we know that in all things God works for the good of those who love him,*
> *who have been called according to his purpose. (Rom. 8:28 NIV)*

Living a life full of purpose can be a humbling journey that sometimes may seem small or insignificant. Fulfilling your life's purpose doesn't always come easy, and sometimes it may even seem like God isn't near, but He is always working for our good. Our job is simple: just continue to put our hope, trust, and love in Him according to Romans 8:28. When we truly learn to love the Lord and trust that God will work it out, then we ultimately submit to His will. We can be confident that no matter what position we are in today, His purpose is what matters forever. Purpose can be found in the deserted places, where life situations may seem to be dry. And it can also be found in the high places, where everything seems to be going right. Your purpose is connected to being in the presence of God and in fellowship with Him through your relationship. Your positions in life should not undermine your relationship with God no matter the hour, season, or location. Simply put, to find purpose is to seek God. We can be assured that God is always present, but it's our job to make him visible.

Some of the best business proposals have come in some of the most unlikeliest places. Take Keijuane Hester, for example, owner of Favor Desserts in my hometown, Durham, North Carolina. His company's slogan is "Pound for pound; we are the best in town." Hester has built a strong reputation in Durham and has rightfully earned the nickname "The Cake Man" because of his delicious five-flavor, red-velvet, and many other delicious cakes. Every time I make a trip home, I'm almost guaranteed to stop by Favor Desserts to purchase those delicious red-velvet cupcakes.

Keijuane Hester has a unique journey that has lead him to becoming a successful businessman. I first got to learn more about his story as a student in Ms. Daye's tenth grade business entrepreneurship class at Hillside High School. Before being popularly known as "The Cake Man," he was tried and convicted of dealing with drugs and sentenced to serve four years in prison. While studies show that rates of recidivism are nearly more than 50 percent, rates have been proven to go down with stable employment. Keijuane Hester was looking not only for stable employment; he was looking to own his next employment once he was released from prison. During his prison sentence, Keijuane Hester found a greater calling in the state penitentiary's kitchen. He developed the love for baking and enjoyed sharing his incredible skills with others.

As we fast-forward to the present day, those baking lessons in prison are now paying off for him in a mighty way. Keijuane Hester now serves the Durham community through his delicious cakes and positive motivational messages. He once told inmates, "It's not about the tool of baking that I want to be remembered by. I want to be known by the transformation that has taken place in my life. I wouldn't be doing what I am doing today if I had not been locked up for selling drugs." Even before Keijuane Hester had the means to own his own store, he had taken and used lessons he learned on the streets to his advantage and had redefined hitting the streets in a more positive way by now selling his delicious cakes. When I was a young man, my barbershop happened to be one of his routine visits. I would always make a point to ask my parents to spare me an extra $5.00 to buy a cake, in case the Cake Man stopped by. I would be so disappointed if I missed him that day. Keijuane Hester believes that his purpose in life is to show that someone who had a negative past could turn it around into a productive life and could earn an honest living.

We've all have made mistakes in life. I urge you to never think that your mistake will cause you to lose out in fulfilling your calling. We serve a gracious God who will meet us where we are and cares more about our eternal purpose than our mistakes. Obviously, our mistakes come with certain consequences and with a price. Although Keijuane Hester had to serve jail time, God was with him and is working all things out for his good. Not only did he leave jail as a free man, he also left as a better man, with a new set of skills that has helped him lead a successful business. With all due respect, if Keijuane Hester could redefine success in his life after all that he had been through, so can we!

Success is about making the most out of your positions with the kingdom's perspective—even if success may not come in the form, size, shape, or color that you once hoped for. It is important that we redefine success and embrace the change that is necessary for growth in Kingdom perspective.

Author's Motivation:
The Ultimate Success Story

What does success look like to God? If heaven has a dictionary with the word success in it, Jesus's picture would be the model for success. In fact, more than likely, He would be the ideal image of many things. Jesus left his heavenly throne to come conquer the world from eternal damnation, bondage, and death. The Bible calls the earth the devil's home, so God's plan of crossing the devil's territory was through the birth of Jesus in the womb of the Virgin Mary. As a man, he lived the perfect life without sin. He endured forty days and forty nights of temptation from the devil, and He used Scripture to lure him to a successful victory. He defeated death on the Cross, evident by yelling out his last words, "Tetelestai" (which means "It is finished"). Three days later, His victory was confirmed after being risen from the grave, leaving the tomb completely empty. Jesus did not do any of this for self-glorification, but He did this as a sacrificial offering for everyone to fulfill their purpose in coming back to God. This is the ultimate success story that will never be redefined. This is the Good News of the gospel and should be our motivation to live a life full of purpose.

CHAPTER 4

POSITION

What does it look like to live full of purpose within your positions in life? When I lived in Bloomington, Indiana, I would often make trips to the local CVS store down the street from my home. There was this one particular store clerk that I would see almost every time. She isn't just any old, ordinary, clock-in-just-to-clock-out, nine-to-five, gloomy clerk. From our first interaction, I knew that there was something different about her, although I couldn't quite figure it out. She is the type of lady who smiles with joy and who is quick to serve if you can't find a certain item. When she opens her mouth, you might as well get ready to add an extra fifteen minutes to your CVS trip, although you came to buy only one item. This lady would talk your head off if you let her, and the only way to be saved, is if someone else was in line behind you. I always enjoyed my conversations with her because of the way she made me feel .

There was something about her that brought me joy, peace, and a sense of family connection. Although I did not know this woman personally, she had a way of making me feel welcome! Our conversations could travel from one place to another as we would discuss novels to read, television shows to watch, what we heard on the inspirational radio, and, somehow, our conversations were always centered around purpose. One particular visit, I asked her if she felt like working at CVS fulfilled her purpose and calling in life. Without hesitation, she responded with great passion, "My purpose in life is to make people laugh; I'm a comedian." Now most people who walk in the store would see a woman behind the cash register, in a blue-collared shirt with a CVS nametag, who finalizes their purchases. But comedian? No way. What I loved about this woman is how she did not allow her job, her title, her location, or her position to define her calling; rather, she defined herself on the basis of her purpose *to make people laugh*. "*A joyful heart is good medicine, But a broken spirit dries up the bones*" (Prov. 17:22 NASB).

Although she doesn't have your typical comedian platform in front of thousands of people, I would claim that she is fulfilling her call to make people smile right there in CVS. Her job is to make an enjoyable and an easy experience for hundreds of daily customers that come into the store. She decides to live a purposeful life over a positional life. No wonder I would gravitate toward her awesome personality and always leave the store with an gratifying experience . Instead of her chasing the comedy stage, she allows her passion to follow her. Most people would try to turn off purpose in environments that do not seem to complement their passion, but a person of purpose walks with deep convictions. Purpose should not be a light switch that turns on and off when you are passionate about maximizing your calling. I am forever grateful for her demonstration of what having passion in purpose looks like and for her display of purpose over position.

You ultimately determine the drive of your position by your values and beliefs, and by choosing to operate in greater purpose over position. Every time that I traveled to the local CVS, I received "good medicine" in spirit, as I left with a cheerful heart because of this purpose-driven worker. This is a woman who has positioned herself with great perspective because she does not allow her job title to define her values and core beliefs.

Positions in God Should Come First

God has given us all the unique ability to control the way that we respond to the positions in our lives. We have the choice to use it for positive gain or negative effect. Maybe you are striving toward becoming a medical doctor, a business owner, a professional athlete, or the next president of the United States . Whatever you are positioning yourself toward, God's agenda is to align you with positions that match His divine kingdom purpose for your life. As we strive to live out our dreams and our goals in life, it is important that we must always be in the constant presence of our Father, God.

Sometimes God deals with your position in Him before He open the doors for anything else. By doing this, you find your true identity, the kingdom's perspective, and your reliance on Him. Life is full of many positions: part-time or full-time, mother or father, husband or wife, employee or employer, wealthy or poor, married or divorced. However, positions in life can oftentimes be misleading. Once you have been given a position or title, people will define you with it. It can often allow one to feel more empowered than another or to feel incompetent because of the status of the positioner.

I know this all too well as an African-American man living in the challenges of prejudice, an unjust system, and racism. The level of misjudgment, misunderstanding, and misuse of the African-American race has been apparent in the unjust American systems and has been recently magnified due to the recent deaths of innocent black lives that have come to light. Racism is nothing new and has been prevalent for a very long time, and the events that continue to arise nationally expose the dark forces behind these efforts. Though we as a nation and world have come a long way, it is disheartening to see any group of people being treated as less than human. Racism and injustice have found their way in all races. As a African American, myself, the bigoted cycle of racism continues to cut deep generationally. I personally have had countless of experiences that have taught me that racism remains deeply rooted in the hearts of so many people.

What I've concluded is that it often comes down to a reverence issue, when one does not value the Creator's creation. Reverence simply just means to have a deep respect for someone or something. The royal law found in James indicates that we should "love our neighbor as we love ourselves." If we would only embrace this law, the demonic force behind racism would come to ruins. However, if we are having a difficult time loving ourselves, then we will have difficulty in our love for God, since we are ultimately created and formed in

His likeness and image, the *imago Dei*. From there, if our hearts are not turned toward the love of God, then it is impossible to love thy neighbor.

Athletics has helped bridge the gap in knocking down the walls of racism, because people idolize athletes and cheer for their favorite sports teams, despite an athlete's color. My experience being an athlete often seemed to be one of only a few ways that African Americans in America are either accepted or celebrated. This is very unfortunate and a hard truth to accept. Therefore, in so many situations, many times, I've had to revert back to my position as an athlete, not only to receive acceptance, but also in hopes of eliminating that thought of me being a threat to my environment because of the color of my skin. I've personally encountered racism on many occasions, especially when my jersey was off and people could no longer associate or identify me with athletics. After my athletic career, the hardest reality personally was no longer receiving the type of acceptance that I once received when the jersey was on. The reality of racism in America has taught me that we must not cling to titles and positions but instead cling to God, who is the heavenly Father to all people groups. As a positive, the world can learn a lot from team sports because they are represented by so much diversity and commitment in unifying individuals from all different walks of life and for one common goal: to win. My prayer is that we all share the locker room of unity as citizens of heaven , "*standing together with one spirit and one purpose, fighting together for the faith, which is the Good News*" (Phil. 1:27 NLT).

As we read the Scripture above, we should see that God highlights the importance of the number one, which represents unity. Jesus taught the disciples that in John 10:30 (NIV): "*I and the Father are one.*" Unity within God's creation is a foundational principle that we all have a part in playing. The Scripture also highlights the importance of fighting together instead of fighting against each other. Any organization or idea that dismisses the idea of unity or fighting together is an empire that will never last. God does not need man's agenda; instead, He invites man to establish His kingdom agenda on Earth. God invites mankind to be in unity with Him. That unity is only exemplified when we are unified within ourselves. Not just the righteous but also the unrighteous. Not just the Republicans but also the Democrats. Not just the rich but also the poor. Not just the straight but also the crooked. Not just one nation but every nation. He wants oneness in all people of His creation, whom He has chosen, to carry His likeness, image, and presence all throughout the Earth.

Positioned for Purpose

The word *position* refers to the environment and the place where a person is to carry out his or her purpose. After I received the message that my college career was over prematurely because of my foot-ligament injury, the position as the starting quarterback was no longer mine; rather, it belonged to JMU all-time great and FCS National Champion Bryan Schor. Although not being able to play was extremely difficult, I had an unbelievable joy that God was up to something big in my life. My position was not all that mattered; rather, it was focusing on God's position in the midst of my storm that became my priority. My life was far from over, and my purpose was bigger than my starting football position. Motivational speaker Brian Tracy once said, " Become the kind of leader that people would follow voluntarily, even if you had no title or position." Now being stripped from my position, I had to make a choice each and every day to not make it about me and my pain. So I dedicated time every week to think about ways to motivate the team during pregame speeches, and I was charged to cover the team during our pregame prayers (see Heb. 10:24 for inspiration). While it took a lot of humility to be on the sideline position, I was in turn able to gain new perspective about the game, about my teammates, and, ultimately, about life that I never would have received had it not been for my new position. I was able to lead from the heart and not just from the emotions that come with the thrill of playing. God positioned me into purpose, which required a new position of servitude and gratitude.

In many sporting events today, there is usually a team chaplain or character coach present to help support the athletes' holistic development. At JMU, we relied on local leaders or pastors to come in to share a word of encouragement, since we did not have a full-time chaplain at the time. Four days after a successful surgery, my coach, Everett Withers, asked me if I would be willing to step into the position of leading inspirational messages with the team, in the same manner as a team chaplain would do. To be completely honest, I was petrified, nervous, and afraid of how my teammates would respond to me in this new position. Thoughts of being laughed at by teammates and the guilt of feeling like I was not worthy enough plagued my mind. I was also worried that the message of the Good News would be hard to receive from a guy who was on crutches and who just lost his senior season, which seemed like the opposite of good news. But what I have come to learn is that God was positioning me for that very moment. God has ultimately revealed that the position itself is not of importance, but the purpose associated with the position at that time is what should be of value. His purpose for my life went far beyond the football field, far beyond being cool with the boys; but suffering has its place to be meaningful encouragement in other people's lives. Once I realized that it was not about me but about glorifying God even in the midst of the biggest trail of my young life, I could not pass up the opportunity to encourage my friends, teammates, and brothers.

If I remember correctly, the title of my very first message to the team was "What is your spiritual position? Starter? Backup? Benchwarmer?" The message was crafted in a way that would be appealing to the crowd of coaches and athletes. I still hold on to that message today as a memory of God positioning me into purpose. That one experience has led me to a career of speaking, ministering, and helping athletes recover from their brokenness. Since then, I have held positions in sports and college ministries as the character coach and spiritual director for several sports teams. Today, I enjoy leading and building up young people and leaders in the community through devotional motivation, similar to my first experience in front of my teammates and coaches. I've become much more confident and polished since my first message. It is pretty amazing how that one act of obedience has transformed into a lifetime of purpose and calling. Since then, I've spoken to several Division I football teams, and I've been even recognized as a potential candidate for similar roles at multiple big-time colleges and NFL football teams. I do not wish to boast but only to encourage that God is always positioning His children for greater purpose. He always knows how to turn a bad thing into a good thing or a good thing into a better thing.

Change Our Thinking

² Now there is in Jerusalem by the Sheep Gate a pool, which is called in Hebrew, [a]Bethesda, having five porches. ³ In these lay a great multitude of sick people, blind, lame, [b]paralyzed, [c]waiting for the moving of the water. ⁴ For an angel went down at a certain time into the pool and stirred up the water; then whoever stepped in first, after the stirring of the water, was made well of whatever disease he had. ⁵ Now a certain man was there who had an infirmity thirty-eight years. ⁶ When Jesus saw him lying there, and knew that he already had been in that condition a long time, He said to him, "Do you want to be made well?"

⁷ The sick man answered Him, "Sir, I have no man to put me into the pool when the water is stirred up; but while I am coming, another steps down before me."

⁸ Jesus said to him, "Rise, take up your bed and walk." ⁹ And immediately the man was made well, took up his bed, and walked. (John 5:2–9 NIV)

For thirty-eight years, this unidentified man found himself in a disadvantaged, unfortunate lame position. I can only imagine how hopeless it must have been for him to be in that condition for so long. I'm sure feelings of confusion, rejection, and frustration often flooded his mind. Despite his condition, Jesus did not identify him as a lame man but instead as an opportunity to empower Him to take on a new position and a new reality. Notice in the passage, Jesus did not say, "I can heal you." Instead, He humbly and confidently asked the man, "Do you want to be made well?" Two important points to take away are:

1. Walking in the kingdom's purpose and dominion does not require convincing or explaining but is a natural flow, like streams of living water. In other words, Jesus did not need to convince this man that He has the power to heal him from his condition because he indeed is *Jehovah-Rapha*, which means "God who heals" in the Hebrew language. He lives and walks in that authority and dominion.

2. Jesus, already knowing of the man's condition and his desire to be healed, only asked as an invitation to offer the man His kingdom's perspective.

This was not only an invitation to heal the lame man's condition, but an invitation to be filled with God's supernatural encounter that will change the course of this man's life forever.

In the kingdom of God, we discover miracles, signs, and wonders. As kingdom citizens, we have access to " heaven on Earth" by walking in the spirit and by asking for permission. Jesus exemplifies a life of the miraculous, that as believers we have access to. Jesus invited the lame man to shift from the natural perspective to the supernatural advantage point by his question that was to bring glory to the Father in heaven, not glory to man. His question was to honor eternal healing, not a paralytic position. His question was to help the man to no longer focus on his position but to look toward his greater purpose. I can only imagine how an encounter like this can impact one's life, faith, and desire to live a life full of purpose. An encounter such as this can change one's perspective from man-centric to God-centric, earth-centric to heaven-centric, position-centric to purpose-centric!

For thirty-eight years, this man was paralyzed and, I'm sure, emotionally drained from the hardships of his reality. But Jesus tends to show up when we might be going through things with no one to help us. Jesus's question to the man demanded a kingdom response. However, much like ourselves, the man knew only to respond out of his emotional disappointment of his circumstance of the last thirty-eight years. *"I have no man to put me into the pool"* (John 5:7). The lame man was not only physically paralyzed; in addition, his condition influenced his way of thinking. Some may find themselves having the same mentality as the lame man in other situations. In order to experience all the benefits of being a kingdom citizen, we must change the way that we think. The Bible declares in Proverbs 23:7 (NKJV): *"for as he thinks in his heart, so is he."* Positions are often reflective of the way you think. For the lame man, his thoughts dictated his response when Jesus offered him healing. For you, it may be a similar circumstance that holds you back from receiving your blessing. The kingdom of God demands change in the way that we think by renewing our perspective on Him daily. Jesus had to redefine the man's perception and thoughts in order to change his condition.

PAUSE MOMENT: Let's take a second to reflect on this topic.

What is a defining situation, condition, or area in your life that can be paralyzing to your spiritual, emotional, and physical growth? Do you want to be made well? How are you renewing your mind to receive greater things from God? As a result, is that helping you to change the way that you think? Discuss with a friend, family member, or small group to have a great dialogue. Jot down in a journal what you have learned from this experience.

I love this redeeming passage of Scripture because in the end, the lame man received more than just a man to help him into the pool and more than just healing, but, after all those years, he received an encounter with Jesus, where he had access to power and strength from above. This man went from having no strength to now having all the strength and power to pick up that same bed that once held his lame body for thirty-eight years. Although it is probably not important, since the Bible doesn't specify, but I personally wonder what the man did with that bed once he received deliverance from being paralyzed. I would imagine that he tossed it into the dump and never wanted to associate himself with that bed again after spending thirty-eight years on it. But oddly enough, sometimes the very thing that we attach ourselves to for so long can be the very thing that's hard for us to actually let go of. I'm sure it wasn't an easy process because change never is. The process of dying to your flesh is never easy, but it is necessary in order to move toward the calling that God has placed on your life. Maybe this will serve as an encouragement to our own life situations. It's time to stop sitting around the pool of Bethesda, hoping and wishing for a miracle. It's time to get up, to take up our position, and to walk toward our destiny. It's time to get a new bed. It's time to change the way that we think.

The Effect of Positions

Position is just another label, and if we are not careful, a position can try to compete with our true identity in life. When one illuminates his/her position over the purposes of God in their hearts is where humanity gets into big trouble with God. Well-known leadership guru John C. Maxwell wrote a must-read leadership book titled, *The 5 Levels of Leadership* . Position is, in fact, one of five levels of maximizing your potential. In the book, he highlights the upside of position as well as the downside of position from a leadership perspective. Position is the only level that does not require ability or effort to achieve. Anyone can be appointed to any position at any given time. The only kicker is that positions are only short-lived and must come to an end at some point.

We all face many positions in life, including positions that we are not necessarily to fond of. I think about my good friend and mentor, Scott Stankavage, who has spent the last six years of his life living with terminal stage-four leukemia. As the father of six beautiful children, including three under the age of eight, there is no time for Scott to allow this temporary circumstance to overcome his eternal fatherhood with his children and partnership with his wife. Besides, even if he did, his younger kids would probably not understand well enough for him to soak in his own emotional battles because they see Daddy as their superhero. Scott, once the former Denver Broncos quarterback behind John Elway and Gary Kubiak, went from fighting for inches on the football field to now fighting for every day of his life. After all, the medical doctors gave him a prediction that he had only five years to live. However, Scott has made a living dodging defenders to keep the play alive, which has served him well in his daily battles with cancer. Every day is a new a day for Scott, and every moment is precious, as he lives on experimental drugs, makes multiple doctor visits a week, and suffers physical exhaustion because of the strenuous procedures he goes through daily. The side effects of his stage-four cancer battle sometimes include severe weight loss, hair loss, and mood swings, and so much more that I cannot even fully comprehend. Scott is a hero of mine, not because he is surviving cancer but because he is not allowing his condition to define who he is and his purpose in life. As a competitor on the field, I did not think there was another level of competitiveness, but Scott has raised the standards as he is kicking cancer straight in the gut. Looking back at the pain that I experienced from my injury during those five months is nowhere near the amount of suffering that Scott has endured over the past five years. Scott is a man of purpose, and he has the heart of an ultimate warrior. I enjoy my time with Scott, and I always expect him to be the funny, upbeat, and relational guy that he is because there is no doubt in my mind that Jesus is making him well.

The New Position

"Therefore, if anyone is in Christ, the new creation has come: The old has gone, the new is here"(1 Cor. 5:17 NIV).

God is always in the right position to move in your life, even if it seems like you are not. In the darkest days, God has proven that He is always ready to dismiss the old and to create us anew. Even for those who may just be exploring the claims of Christ, you have the opportunity to be transformed into a new creation. Choosing Christ is accepting and inviting His presence into your life. Christ has the power to transform our minds, our hearts, and our lives through His holiness. When we decide to accept Him, we no longer worry about our position on Earth, but instead enhance our focus to live in the new position worthy of eternity. That's why dwelling in the Holy Bible is important for our mind, our character, or our emotion each and every day. A good barometer of a person's life is the amount of time he or she spends hearing, reading, sharing, and discussing the Word of God. When your life is being transformed by the gospel, your new position begins to be transformed by Christ and His Word. This is apparent in Joshua 1:8 (BSB) that says, *"This Book of the Law must not depart from your mouth, meditate on it day and night, so that you may be careful to do everything written in it. For then you will prosper and succeed in all you do."* Do you want to prosper and succeed in all that you do? Wait, is that even possible? According to this Scripture, if we would just live our lives through God's Holy and divine Word then no longer would we question His ways in our lives. If there is one Scripture that we should apply to memory and action, it is Joshua 1:8.

Take Up Your Position

Are you fighting for victory, or are you operating out of victory? Philip Anthony Mitchell, the pastor of Victory Church ATL, often reminds the congregation that if we are truly positioning ourselves as Christ's followers, then we must "operate in a place of victory and not fighting for victory." I love this reminder because in the same way, we should operate in our God-given purpose instead of fighting for humanity's position. The story has already been written for humanity to experience true purpose from the Creator. Therefore, the creation can only get purpose from the Creator. Second Chronicles 20:17 (NLT) validates this message of encouragement : "*But you will not even need to fight. Take up your positions; then stand still and watch the Lord's victory.*" Taking up your position is an act of worship unto God. Your position is not just to sit around waiting, but it is to stand alongside of Him, while He moves with you, through you, and for you. Stand still in His presence, knowing that the enemy can't frighten you with his cycled tactics. I think about the image of the late, great Kobe Bryant, who stood his ground without flinching when one of his opponents pretended to throw the ball directly at his face. Bryant did not even blink; he took up his position and stood his ground. Many of us would have been quick to flinch from the threat of an object being thrown at our face. However, Kobe in his *mamba mentality* took up his position and stood his ground without fear. Faith over fear is what allows us to remain in position with God, even in the midst of battle. Position yourself in a place where God sees you standing with boldness and confidence because you have indeed already won the victory.

Author's Motivation:
Purpose over Pandemic

While the 2020 global COVID-19 pandemic changed the entire world forever, it's important that we learn from that season of life. Many of us who lived through the pandemic lost family members, jobs, relationships, church members, and maybe even our connection with God. Some studies have shown that divorce rates have spiked, and the number of family violence cases increased as a result of so many people struggling to cope with the new normal inside of their homes. The pandemic ruined a lot of plans: weddings, graduations, high school proms, school outings, sporting events, and so much more. It is the beginning of the end for a lot of businesses, plans, and dreams. In the midst of so much bad news, we can always turn to the Good News in Jesus's story of redemption. Though we are looking forward to the day of living without fear of setbacks, the psalmist in Psalm 121 (KJB) reminds us to "lift up mine eyes unto the hills, from whence cometh my help. My help cometh from the Lord, which made heaven and earth." Evaluate what your eyes have been fixed on during difficult days and hardships.

Perhaps your focus is on the news, political debates, or all your friends' opinions on social media platforms. Fixing our eyes on these places can create a massive amount of depression, frustration, and a sense of unfulfillment. God cares deeply about the things that we are dealing with during our troubled times. However, the psalmist encourages us to look into the kingdom solutions when we need help. It is not kingdom-like for us to continue to keep our eyes fixed on the problem, but it is when our eyes are fixed upon God. Having your eyes down is a sign of defeat or surrender to something or someone other than God. Though it may be tempting and easy to give up to the deadly and invisible demonic forces, be encouraged, even in your current position. Let's fix our eyes on God's kingdom where greater purpose over pandemics resides.

CHAPTER 5

OPPOSITION

Have you ever been on board of an airplane? Takeoff is one of my favorite parts. Sitting on the runway, waiting for the plane to pick up speed, almost never gets old for me. After learning the science behind the take-off on the runway, you'll discover that in order for an airplane to take off, it must first create opposition with the wind. The reason why the airplane gets louder as it picks up speed on the runway is because the wind beats up against the aircraft in opposition. Oddly enough, the opposition of air actually helps lift the aircraft by positioning the air underneath the wings for liftoff. This is great imagery as we think about our own lives in how to best approach opposition. In our lives, we must not allow opposition to bind us in chains of fear and regret. Your life is guaranteed to attract opposition, especially when you are striving to live a holy lifestyle. Much like the airplane, we must remember that opposition is sometimes necessary to lift us up to new heights. Some of the best ideas, thoughts, and creations have been born out of times of setback.

Fulfilling the purpose you were created for in life is one of the most rewarding things that a human being will experience during their existence.

When you realize that your dreams are just one block away, one bold sacrifice away, or one divine prayer away, your pursuit of purpose will be fulfilled. But here's the warning: when you are walking within the fulfillment of your God-given purpose in life, you need to learn how to deal with opposition. The best way to learn how to live an empowered life is to learn how the Lord dealt with opposition. When Satan came to Adam and Eve in the beginning, he came in the form of a serpent. He challenged Eve by opposing what God instructed them to do. Let's take a look.

> [1] Now the serpent was more crafty than any other beast of the field that the LORD God had made. He said to the woman, "Did God actually say, 'You shall not eat of any tree in the garden'?" [2] And the woman said to the serpent, "We may eat of the fruit of the trees in the garden, [3] but God said, 'You shall not eat of the fruit of the tree that is in the midst of the garden, neither shall you touch it, lest you die.'" [4] But the serpent said to the woman, "You will not surely die. [5] For God knows that when you eat of it your eyes will be opened, and you will be like God, knowing good and evil." (Gen. 3:1 ESV)

Of course we go on to read as a result of this conversation, Adam and Eve decided to eat the forbidden fruit, and as punishment, humanity became indulged in sin. Sin is what separates humanity from God. Without the ministry and ultimate sacrifice of Jesus's death and resurrection, there would be no way for a sinner to be in the presence of God, which hints as to why Jesus is the only and true way to enter heaven's gates. Satan thrives in the spirit of deception and lies that make people stumble along the way of life. Therefore, it is imperative that we remain sharp in His Word and presence.

When Jesus first began His ministry, He was led by the Holy Spirit to fast in the wilderness. During this time, He was tempted by the devil for forty days and forty nights. I call this spiritual training because every believer will be faced with tests in order to strengthen their faith. If you grew up hating tests like I did, you may have built a negative connotation or perception. Maybe you thought the teacher was mean, unfair, or wanted to see you fail. On the other hand, if you took your studies seriously and were prepared for the test, you might have a different outlook. Jesus never folded or gave in to the devil's tricks when he showed up with a test; instead, His answer was rather simple, "It is written." This key to living a life full of purpose is to live according to the Word of God. Notice this response was completely different from Adam and Eve's response to their test in the garden. They both entertained the devil's ideas of opposition and in turn failed the test. Jesus dismissed him right from the start. It's important that we do not entertain the devil's opposition or new ideas like eating the fruit but that we prepare ourselves with the only answer that matters —the Word of God.

Dodging Punches

In the sport of boxing, many spectators focus a lot of attention on the quick left jabs, the powerful haymaker, and the famous uppercuts. While that may be exciting to watch, something we do not value as much is when a fighter is really good at dodging the opponent's punches. In order to be a good boxer, you must develop the art of dodging those famous haymakers and jabs. It takes a skillful individual to obtain the discipline, the focus, and the swiftness to be able to evade 100 mph punches that are meant to knock you out. Muhammad Ali, one of the most celebrated boxing figures, would mesmerize crowds with his swift defensive evasions, and his dance-like boxing style. Of course he was known for his major knockout punches, but what made him great was he was a master defending himself from taking big hits. When a boxer evades an opponent's punch, it increases the chances for the boxer to survive, to remain unharmed, and ultimately, to win. As citizens of the kingdom, you get to frustrate the enemy's plans by being equipped with the necessary skills and knowledge on when to dodge. In life, we may find ourselves in the ring with so much opposition trying to take his best shot. The more we become empowered in our training through God's Word, the more we gain the knowledge and wisdom to know exactly where our opponent's next jab will come from. Therefore, God prepares us to duck, slip, and dodge in order to discern God's plan to live a life full of purpose.

As stated earlier in this book, as believers, we do not fight for victory, but we fight from a position of victory. Even without ever having to throw a punch, we will win because of the authority that we carry through the Word of

God! Staying equipped to get into the ring is important for our overall growth. This is evident in the life of Job, though he went through a major crisis, God covered him in victory. I love how God put the devil in his place by telling him that he had better "not lay a finger" on his servant Job. After taking Satan's best uppercuts, Job came out victorious in the end. (See Job 1:12 NIV.)

Opposition from the Enemy

A wise man once stated that if there is no opposition from the enemy, then you should be worried because if he is not messing with you, then he must have gotten you on his side. So the next time that you want to yell at your boss or to win the argument with your spouse, ask yourself, "What is the purpose here? Even when a person wins the argument, who am I trying to please? Myself or God?" Who is truly getting the glory? God or Satan?"

I love it when lives are being transformed, when the gospel is being preached in new territory, and when people begin to explore the claims of Christ. While ministry is thriving, I become aware of opposition from the enemy. Only when things seem to be going really well and when ministry is thriving, the enemy shows up to oppose. What is most surprising is oftentimes we look for the enemy to be wearing a different color uniform, when in reality, he may be on our own team. Eve influenced Adam to sin , Saul tried to kill David because of his anointing, and Judas was one of Jesus's disciples that betrayed Him and led him to His arrest, ultimately to His death on the cross. While I am not claiming that these individuals were the enemy, they at least once acted under the influence of the enemy. We must be aware that the enemy likes to use deception to sneak inside.

Apostle Paul introduces this to us in the Scriptures by teaching the reality of persecution. From my experience, persecution can be signs and evidence of true gospel ministry being preached. When you are fulfilling your divine purpose that aligns with the will of God for your life, expect persecution to come knocking at the door. The apostle Paul had shipwrecked three times, been stoned for death, had made frequent visits to prison, received the Jewish forty lashes five times, and had suffered even more punishments.

Leaders Embrace Moments of Adversity

Zig Ziglar, a famous author and motivational speaker once shared that "sometimes adversity is what you need to face, in order to become successful." This quote from Ziglar is one that I personally resonate with because it is a total mind shift that helps one to appropriately channel adverse situations for purposeful growth. When adversity comes our way, we must be reminded that our purpose is greater than the current adverse situation or position.

Adversity in a human life is inevitable, and it can either make or break you. A sign of a true leader is preparing to embrace moments of crisis. In the face of adversity, leaders have the opportunity to become spiritual giants ready to dominate. However, that is only possible if we prepare ourselves to rise up before being faced with the conflict. For example, David pleaded with King Saul to let him take out the earthly giant, Goliath.

> [34] But David said to Saul, "Your servant has been keeping his father's sheep. When a lion or a bear came and carried off a sheep from the flock, [35] I went after it, struck it and rescued the sheep from its mouth. When it turned on me, I seized it by its hair, struck it and killed it. [36] Your servant has killed both the lion and the bear; this uncircumcised Philistine will be like one of them, because he has defied the armies of the living God. [37] The Lord who rescued me from the paw of the lion and the paw of the bear will rescue me from the hand of this Philistine." (1 Sam. 17:34–36 NIV)

David's leadership was on display to all the frightened men surrounding him, including the king, Saul. Leaders know the art of channeling their fear. Leaders are those who do not succumb to their fear for the sake of not hindering those who follow their lead. David, a true leader and warrior, was operating in another dimension from all the other trained soldiers, who were petrified of Goliath. David became a spiritual giant that day in his relentless pursuit to dominate his opponent. I get chills just reading this passage, because I can almost feel David's passion pertaining to his preparation. Sometimes we are working in silent excellence, which can actually prepare us to take down giants in our own lives.

David had become equipped with the necessary skills, tools, weapons, and knowledge by the private victories that led to his big public defeat of Goliath. Can you imagine killing a lion or a bear with your bare hands? With those victories under his belt, it almost seems as if squaring off with Goliath seem like no big task after all. David's resilience to work in silent excellence helped him to fulfill his kingdom purpose in his life. God honored David's service to his flock of sheep and no matter what humbling position you are in today, God will honor your kingdom purpose, too. Just keep being humble, even to the point of embracing boredom because a lot of excitement is headed your way. It may not come in the form of a Goliath, but life has a tendency to deal us both good and bad hands. Only you determine the outcome of your walk with obstacles.

Obstacles are a necessary part of growth in humanity. Abraham and Sarah faced adversity after trying countless times to conceive a child. Without this adversity and obstacle in their lives, they would have never experienced the power of God in the birth of their a child at ninety-nine years old. Job faced an enormous amount of adversity after losing all of his children and property in the same day. Even in the midst of so much pain, God would reveal himself to Job as Comforter and would bless him with double anointing.

The Devil tries to keep you far away from God's Word because he understands that calling on the name of Jesus and proclaiming the Scriptures reflect the image of God. When we operate in the Word of God, we, in turn, reflect the Word of God and speak the Word of God. Your past obstacles cannot define your future and who you are. The enemy has no room to dictate the direction in which God is leading you. For this reason, the Bible highlights the importance of putting on the full spiritual armor of God to protect you in the battles of life.

Full Armor of God
Belt of Truth

As we equip ourselves with the armor of God, we no longer face opposition on our own strength but instead God's supernatural strength (see Eph. 6:10–18).

Wearing the belt of truth allows us to stand upright on the truth of God's Word. In the natural world, wearing a belt is used to help secure or hold up clothing. It is commonly used around the waist so that a person's pants do not sag or fall down. I remember that, one day, I forgot to wear a belt to school, and my sagging pants was a major distraction in my day. I found myself pulling up my pants with every transition and sometimes to the point where I had to physically hold on to my jeans to prevent them from falling down. As I dealt with the discomfort of potentially having my backsides exposed to the entire school, I thought to myself that if only I had my belt, not only would my pants be secure, but my self-confidence would be assured as well .

In spiritual fashion, God's truth will set you free from any bondage, opposition, or lie of the enemy. The belt of truth allows you to be spiritually equipped, empowered, and engaged with the purpose of God through the Holy Spirit. The Bible refers to the devil as the "*Father of lies*" (John 8:44), so being covered by the belt of truth will help you to be more aware of godly truths and to overcome the lies of the enemy. You are not dumb; you are smart. You are not forgotten; you are God's chosen. You are more than enough, because God created you in His likeness. You will win, because God has already won. You are not alone, for God has promised that He will always be with you.

The Breastplate of Righteousness

Righteousness comes from the blood of Jesus Christ's sacrifice on the cross of Calvary. When we accept Jesus Christ in our lives, we are justifiable to God through His Son's perfect sacrifice. A breastplate protects the chest. The chest protects the heart. When a person puts on the breastplate of righteousness, they are ready to enter the danger zones of war. We are in the midst of a spiritual war zone each and every day for our hearts, minds, and souls. In this spiritual armor, Christ represents the breastplate with which He is tasked to protect the hearts of the righteous. Righteousness is having the faith and obedience to do whatever God instructs us to do. It is a transformation of the heart for all of those who believe.

The Shoes of Peace

The shoes of peace allow you to stand firm, no matter how hard life gets or how much suffering the enemy throws at you. When you wear the shoes of peace, they allow you to stand firmly and confidently, while the Holy Spirit fights for you. Even if your world may seem a little chaotic, your spirit is unmovable because you have on the shoes of peace to withstand the rain. Walking throughout life has its everyday challenges but the shoes of peace help you to endure to the end. Though you may get weary and tired from the journey and you may encounter some setbacks, you remain in total peace. When your walk is consistently and faithfully in line with the peace of God, no amount of darkness can throw you off your destination. Today and every day, prepare your feet to enter the shoes of peace.

The Shield of Faith

Your faith determines the outcome of the battle and ultimately your life. Hebrews 11:1 (NIV) says, "*Now faith is the confidence that what we hope for and assurance about things we cannot see.*" As a quarterback, every time I drop back to throw the ball, I am at my best when I operate by faith : faith in the play call from my coach , faith in my offensive line to protect me from the defenders , and faith in my wide receivers to get open and catch the pass. The ultimate faith comes when I release the ball. Once the ball leaves my fingertips, the ball must speed into a space where only my wide receiver can reach. Accuracy is a state of mind. You must be able to throw the ball into a space the moving target does not quite yet fill but can meet the ball at the right time. In order to get good at it, it takes a lot of practice, and a lot of faith. We must shield our faith so that we are not easily influenced by any new religion, new idea, or new thought.

The Helmet of Salvation

"*For as he thinks in his heart, so is he*" (Prov. 23:7 NKJV). You are what you constantly think about or focus on. The helmet of salvation is designed to protect your head in battle. When the enemy wants to kill you quickly, he starts by taking away your hope, your peace, your memory, and your thoughts. It's vitally important to renew your mind daily on the promises and premises of God. Salvation comes only by the kingdom of God, and when you are covered by His helmet, you can withstand the unexpected blows of life. In football, we wear helmets to protect our brains from concussions and collisions that could be detrimental to our mental well-being. Although we may still feel the impact and force of the collision, we have a better chance of withstanding the major head injuries that could complicate our health.

The Sword of the Spirit

A sword is designed to kill or to tear apart. I was reading Michael Thompson's book, *The Heart of a Warrior*, in which he writes: "A man carrying a sword would signify he is both armed and dangerous. During times of the Bible, the Roman Empire and well into the Middle Ages, these 'weapons' were wielded by oriented men who were equipped for battle. Isn't it interesting that the one weapon in the Armor of God that is both offensive and defensive is the sword of the spirit?" God has provided the believer with this weapon so we are prepared in battle. The sword therefore is *"not against flesh and blood, but against the rulers, against the authorities and against the powers of this dark world and against the spiritual forces of evil in the heavenly realms"* (Eph. 6:12 NIV).

Timing and Opportunity

"There is a time for everything and a season for every activity (or opportunity) under the heavens" (Eccl. 3:1 NIV). Two things that we cannot undervalue are timing and opportunity. Sometimes you may have the right opportunity but not the right timing. Maybe even true vice versa. This means that you can be a great leader but not have anyone to lead. You can be a great author but not yet have any books to show. You can be an anointed singer but do not have a stage to sing on. You can be a talented athlete but not have a team to play for .

Just because this may not be the season that you were once hoping for, God is always empowering you to receive greater, especially in the present season. If you can hold on to God's promises even in the midst of these behind-the-scenes moments, God will reveal His plans for you at the right time and right opportunity. As I experienced this in my own life, I've come to realize that when timing meets opportunity, you can then be positioned for advancement. God strategically opens doors that He may not necessarily want us to go through but instead wants us to reap the benefits that are associated with the doors being open. Some of those benefits could be lifetime friendships or partnerships, new career discoveries, new lessons or experiences, divine connections, but, ultimately, having access is key.

In the same way, as believers, we must understand the power of having access to the kingdom of God. What you have access to is what you will reap. Daniel understood how to access God's kingdom in the lion's den; David understood how to access God's kingdom against Goliath; Moses understood how to access God's kingdom by freeing the Israelites from slavery. When Jesus began his public ministry, his very first message was, *"Repent, for the Kingdom of God is at hand"* (Matt. 4:17 ESV). As believers, we have access to operate in the kingdom's authority. We can be empowered by God's kingdom by calling on Him to intervene in our daily lives and to lead the way. There are all types of benefits—such as love, joy, peace, patience, kindness, goodness, faithfulness, gentleness, self-control, and healing—that are easily accessible to those who understand their legal rights to access the kingdom of God (See Gal. 5:22-23).

Author's Motivation:
More than Enough

In the modern day, many people try to define and limit someone's giftedness based on their profession. For example, when athletes speak out on social injustice issues and political opinions, they are often told to just "shut up and dribble" or "shut up and play." This type of language discredits the athlete's viewpoint outside of their field of play. This phrase has been thrown around to downgrade the knowledge and intellect of the actual person behind the jersey. Just like this example, I'm sure we all can pinpoint areas in our lives where we have been told that we are not good enough, or our opinion is of little value. Despite the negative, be encouraged because you are more than enough and more qualified than you know because you have been chosen as a beloved son or daughter of the most high King. Do not allow the world to tell your story or dictate your role in impacting the earth. Jesus, as the ultimate leader of character, chooses to build on what we can do instead of focusing on what the world tells us we can't do. God has equipped and called us for a greater work of eternity outside of our work environment. Therefore, you are more than enough to accomplish anything in life that the Lord puts in your journey to fulfill. We are to operate outside of the influence of the world as we are reminded by Jesus to remember that "you do not belong to the world, but I have chosen you out of the world" (John 15:19).

CHAPTER 6

SCOREBOARD

All athletes and sports fans are familiar with the scoreboard; it keeps track of their team's points. Arguably, one of the main features of a scoreboard is the clock. Depending on the score, the clock can be your enemy ; if your team is losing, with limited time remaining or, on the flip side, it could be your friend if your team is winning as the time winds down to end the game. The scoreboard tells the truth about the game because the scoreboard has no emotions or favorites. Once time runs out, there will be one winner and one loser on the basis of the scoreboard. I've seen many players in tears, just staring at the scoreboard, and I've also seen many players smiling with anticipation of the clock ticking down to the final second. I've been on both sides of the spectrum: the agony of defeat and the joy of winning. Time is a commodity that we can never get back. Oftentimes, spectators and fans reflect on the game in terms of what should have and could have happened, but, in reality, their reflections cannot change the outcome. Life is like playing a sports game: some plays will result in success, while other plays may result in a negative outcome. Our job is to make the most of the time that is remaining in our lives to score big. Each day is precious as we will never have a chance to go back.

Progression over Perfection

Although the scoreboard is very important, the lessons learned throughout the game is what's valued the most. Whether you are a player on the winning team or losing team, both teams always elect to go back and reflect on their performance through film study and evaluation. Head football coach at Georgia Tech, Paul Johnson, would always say, "It is never as good as good or bad as bad as it may seem." Watching film made me realize that this was indeed true. When you win the game and play well, you often feel really good about your performance. Maybe even as if you had done everything right. When you lose a game, you may feel like the worst player in history. However, once you turn on the unbiased film you realize that even in a winning performance, there is still room to improve. And in a losing performance, the film may show that you didn't do as bad as you originally felt in the moment. Film study is a visible reflection that helps athletes to reach a level of progression, not perfection .

Reflection gives us an opportunity to imply meaning to our past moments in life. Many times, we hear the phrase, "practice makes perfect." But being perfect in anything in life is truly impossible. The pursuit of perfection only guarantees disappointments along the way. Perfection indicates a flawless state where everything is right. Progression, on the other hand, is moving forward toward a destination, no matter if you win or lose. Your progress in life may never end up in the perfection category, but it's being able to look back to see how far you have come that really counts.

If you are familiar with the video game *Madden*, then you may be familiar with the "Create A Player" feature that gives users the option to create a player of their likeness on the video game. This mode in *Madden* historically has always been one of the most popular features. Growing up, my friends and I would create our players' rating on all ninety-nine, which was the highest rating that one could possibly have. For example, the speed, the throwing power, the tackling, the blocking, and the catching would all be a perfect rating of ninety-nine. This was basically cheating because we all knew that it is quite impossible for any player to be that perfect in real life. And although I have been guilty of creating my player at ninety-nine one or two times before, I eventually recognized that playing the game was not as enjoyable with a perfect player as much it was playing with a progressive player. Playing with my ninety-nine athlete only created false hope and unrealistic expectations in real life once I found out that I had some skills that were not so perfect.

When I began to create my player realistically and left room for progress, I found the game much more enjoyable to play. Although it was more challenging, it helped me to build a game plan around my skill sets, both strengths and weakness. Instead of dominating the game with a perfect player, I began to master my skill sets, even with imperfections. So once you play long enough, those weakness eventually become strengths. Progress may not be shown on the scoreboard, but it is certainly shown in the results.

Your life is a personal scoreboard. You may not see it or even know the score, but God is clocking every minute of your life, every word that comes out of your mouth, and every good or bad decision that you make. Every home run, touchdown, goal, or made shot, God documents it on your personal scoreboard. *"For we must all appear before the judgment seat of Christ, so that each one may receive what is due for what he has done in the body, whether good or evil"* (2 Cor. 5:10 ESV). This verse from the Scriptures indicates that God has a spiritual scoreboard on our lives that shows we will have to one day stand before judgment. The scoreboard determines a winner and a loser, but, in this case, our spiritual scoreboard determines life or death.

PAUSE MOMENT: Let's take a second to reflect on this topic.

Take a moment to reflect. Are you living a purposeful life worthy of a winning outcome? Do you have confidence that your score reflects the glory of God and a life that is destined for eternity? Whether your answers are confident or a bit shaky, God has sent us Good News through redemption of Jesus Christ!

God cares about your progress! God cares about you being on the winning team when the clock strikes zero. He already called in the winning play, which was sending His son Jesus to Earth! Jesus is like the relief pitcher in baseball that comes in to close out the game in order to solidify the win. I remember growing up watching my favorite baseball team, the New York Yankees. Every time the Yankees had the lead in the last few innings, the coaches would call for future Hall of Famer, Manny Rivera, to solidify their lead and close out the game with the win. Each time Rivera took the mound, everyone was sure that the Yankees would come out victorious. It seemed like every time they put him in to finish the game, you had a strong sense that counted as an automatic win. I like to think of Jesus as the closing pitcher in our salvation. The Bible even calls Him *"the author and finisher of our faith"* (Heb. 12:2 NKJV). Jesus is the automatic win for the souls of those who repent and who believe He is the way, the truth and the life.

Winning and Learning

"Consider it pure joy, my brothers and sisters, whenever you face trials of many kinds, because you know that the testing of your faith produces perseverance" (James 1:2–3 NIV). Although life can be tough at times and we go through various trials and tribulations, it is important for us to follow the instructions in the epistle of James. How can we count it all joy, even if the scoreboard doesn't seem to be in our favor? Well, as we embrace the teachings of Jesus, we realize that Jesus did not come to condemn us; rather, He came to teach us and to show us the way. His life was more than a Sunday sermon; it was, at large, a blueprint for humanity in accordance with God. Although the scoreboard determines a winner and a loser, Christ determines winning and learning. When you accept Christ in your life, you cannot lose, no matter the opponent and no matter the trial. You have an opportunity to learn with a joyful heart that trials will help produce endurance in all areas of your life. Jesus doesn't allow us to sink our heads in losses with bitterness but, instead, will use loss as a teachable moment for our ultimate good (Rom. 8:28).

Misuse of Purpose

Purpose misused or misunderstood is a missed opportunity in one's life. Dr Myles Munroe shares, "Where purpose is unknown, abuse is inevitable." If the purpose of marriage is unknown, divorce rates will spike, and families will have a hard time staying together. If the purpose of a job position is unclear to the employee, then he will not have much success with the company. If a person does not understand the purpose of money, then he will ultimately mishandle his money through careless spending. Abuse is to use something for a bad effect or for a bad purpose. If we are able to understand and appreciate the purpose of a thing or person, then we will have the ability to operate entirely in purpose over position.

The Yankees organization did an unbelievable job in managing Manny Rivera. Rivera will go down as one of the all-time greatest pitchers to ever play Major League Baseball. Though he wasn't called on to pitch for many innings in the game, he was precisely utilized at the right time, which was mostly in the last couple endings during a close game. You want to talk about pressure. Imagine having a career where your main job responsibility is to seal the deal. For most of us, that would be way too much of a spotlight to perform our best. The good thing is, if you win the game, then you get all the glory; the bad thing is if you lose, you will inherit all the blame .

Manny Rivera was at his absolute best during these times. Of course he had some tough games that did not always go in his favor but I only remember him being called out of the dugout to save the day. He in fact has a record high of 652 saves throughout his career. Upon on how good he was, Rivera could have easily pleaded to his coaches for more playing time, pitches on the mound, or career starts. However, he set the standard for relief pitchers with unprecedented consistency and efficiency as a key component to the Yankees dynasty of the 1990s and 2000s. Rivera was more effectively used for greater purpose in two of the most important innings instead of being average for the first seven innings. Much like this Manny Rivera example, true purpose has a level of intentionality and consistency that a person thrives in which enhances the entire organization. The Yankees understood that they had an exclusive advantage in Rivera, a clutch factor. They won many games because of their discipline in keeping him fresh until it was time to secure the bag. If they had misused his abilities, they would have inevitably done both him and themselves a great disservice.

Work the Field

Working the field requires the Word of God to be alive and active in your life. God gave man purpose by positioning him exactly where He wanted man to thrive. Even before Eve was created, God gave Adam instructions to work and to take care of the field in the Garden of Eden. This reminds me when I began working my job as a security officer, I realized the importance of taking care of someone else's property. My role as a security officer included duties, such as having a watchful eye, upholding the integrity of the company, and making sure everything was in its proper place. Because I often worked during nontraditional hours, the employees at the building were not usually on site, so, in a way, I was much like Adam tending to the garden alone. The one major request that was demanded of me from the building manger was to "please take care of my building." Her main concern was similar to God's intention for man, *"to tend and watch over it"* (Gen. 2:15 NLT). Another way to interpret what God told Adam and what the manager told me is to secure and protect. If anything was to happen to the building, that responsibility would ultimately fall on me because of my failure to secure and protect. This explains why God sought out Adam instead of Eve when they disobeyed God's order of not eating the fruit (Gen. 3:6–15). God went after the man first because He gave the man the responsibility to secure and protect. I thank God for my security job because it taught me the value of God's original intent for men to guard and protect their positions as husbands, fathers, pastors, athletes, entrepreneurs, leaders, and all that are in His care.

The First Will Be the Last; the Last Will Be the First

One of my favorite recorded moments in sports happened in the 1992 Barcelona Olympics. USA runner Derek Redmond was the favorite to win the opening 400-meter dash. But, about 200 meters within the race, tragedy happened. Derek Redmond tore his right hamstring, causing him to drop out of the race. As he fell to the ground, he screamed in agony and pain from a pulled hamstring injury. On top of the physical hurt, I'm sure that his heart sank in deep disappointment, after years of training so hard for this moment. But Derek Redmond didn't give himself time to soak in his puddle of tears or to drown in disappointing thoughts; instead, he got back up to finish the race. As the other runners finished up, Derek Redmond hobbled around the track on one leg, determined to finish what he had been working so hard for. With tears running down his face and his right leg dragging on the track, Derek became an instant hero to the world of sports fans that were watching. Derek Redmond displayed what it was like to have joy in a disappointing moment.

Although the scoreboard was against him, he never gave up. His time may go down as the slowest time in Olympic 400-meter history, but the important thing is that he got back up. Proverbs 24:16 (NIV) states , *"for though the righteous fall seven times, they rise again."* Much like when a toddler is discovering his/her ability to walk on their own strength, with each step they are bound to tumble over heading for a major fall. Their eagerness and excitement to get back up is what makes the process enjoyable. Just like babies, in life, we are all bound to fall sometimes, but if your faith is in the Lord, you do not settle for the ground but instead get back up again. We were never meant to stay down. Although we might not understand or make sense of tough positions, we can be confident in our ability to get back up. Redmond could not control his hamstring injury, but what he could control was his response to rise again. When reflecting on disappointing moments in life, there is always a blessing associated with them, if only you find a way to get back up and walk righteously with God.

Matthew 20:16 (KJV) tells us, *"So the last shall be first, and the first last: for many be called, but few chosen."* On paper, Redmond finished last that day, but he became first in effort, first in spirit, and first in the hearts of a lot of people. The greatest thing about Redmond's story is that he didn't have to suffer around the track alone. A certain spectator came running out of the crowd, breaking through security to run onto the track to help Redmond finish the race. That unknown spectator at the time was later identified as his father! Once he finally got to his son, Redmond was just about halfway to the finish line.

Redmond's father helped his son hobble around the track so that he could finish the race. They both received a well-deserved standing ovation in front of 65,000 people in attendance. If Redmond had given up or if he had stayed down in defeat or if he had felt sorry for himself, his father would have never had the opportunity to help his son reach the finish line. This can easily serve as an image of us and our Father in heaven when we press on, despite life circumstances. Jesus is there among the crowd, praying for you, empowering you, strengthening you, and guiding you to the finish line. The name *Imman-uel* means "God with us." So no matter if you feel down and out or if you are feeling that your back is against the wall, have confidence and faith that God is always with us, looking for opportunities to help each and every one of us to endure to the end. The scoreboard may not always play out like we want it to, but your reward is from the Lord. Do not ever give up on your life and the purpose God created you for. Matthew 24:13 (NKJV) says, *"But he who endures to the end shall be saved."*

The Kingdom's Call

If you are reading this, there is still time left on the scoreboard. To all who may be weary, unsure about in getting in the game, Coach God is dialing up a play just for you. Listen in closely to the play call that has been passed along to Quarterback Jesus and now to you. Here's the play call for your soul, salvation, and repentance: *"If you confess with your mouth, "Jesus is Lord," and believe in your heart that God raised him from the dead, you will be saved"* (Rom. 10:9 NIV).

Ready, break!

Confession is simply repentance of your sins. Did you confess with your mouth that "Jesus is Lord"? Do you believe in your heart that Jesus is Lord? Do you believe in God's power to raise Jesus from the dead? Do you believe that this is the greatest comeback story in history of comebacks? If you answered "Yes" to all of these questions, then you are now a part of God's eternal kingdom. Praise God! You were once covered in sin, but now you are dripping with the glory of the Lord Jesus Christ. You have joined the ultimate victory! All the L's (lessons) that you have experienced in your past have ultimately been leading you to this very moment. The scoreboard will now and forever be in your favor for eternal life as long as you remain faithful. Congratulations! Your biggest fans are in heaven rejoicing with you and for you before the throne of the Lord (See Luke 15:7). For those that are already a part of the body of Christ, keep lighting the scoreboard up! God is pleased to see that His Word sustains the seasoned saints and empowers the new believers for greater.

Author's Motivation: The N.F.L.

At the beginning of 2018, my wife surprised me to tears with a gift so meaningful and cherished, even still today. It was my very first personal Bible with my name engraved on the cover. On the outside of the Bible is a leather-gripped Bible cover that feels like the texture of an actual football. In big letters are the letters, N.F.L. These letters are most commonly used as an abbreviation for the National Football League. However, for my Bible cover, N.F.L is abbreviated for New Found Life. I've never been that emotional over a gift before, but that gift was symbolic for dying to my own fleshly desires as I humbly submit to God's ultimate purpose in Christ .

When we put Jesus before our own desires, it causes us to break free from the things that we really want and pursue what we really need. Although I always wanted to play in the NFL, I desperately needed a new-found life in Christ. That gift put so much in perspective for me as I embraced the new-found life acronym. We all have the opportunity to live a new-found life with Jesus Christ. I can only imagine what draft day in heaven will look like for the believer. With the number one pick in the New-Found Life, Coach Jesus selects (insert your name), to enter the eternal kingdom of God. Can you imagine how you might feel as you walk across stage, hearing the words "Well done, my good and faithful servant"?

CHAPTER 7

ETERNITY

W hen we reflect on life and imagine the glory of God, it will all lead us back toward eternity with our Creator. God has promised a life of eternity with Him if we choose to follow Him. Jesus teaches His disciples in John 14:1–3 (NIV): *"Do not let your hearts be troubled. You believe in God; believe also in me. ² My Father's house has many rooms; if that were not so, would I have told you that I am going there to prepare a place for you? ³ And if I go and prepare a place for you, I will come back and take you to be with me that you also may be where I am."* Our purpose is connected to the one and true savior, Jesus Christ. If we become or remain eternally focused on Him, no position or opposition can take us away from being in purpose. No matter what your situation may look like around you, the challenges can be in response to your kingdom's advancement.

Commissioned

Think about and truly evaluate your life positions. Were you called to the profession that you are in right now? Or, did you see an opportunity that you were qualified to fill? I'm not sure if I've been called to a certain job, position, or location. However, I am sure that my purpose is connected to His eternal commission to go, since our purpose is in His presence. From my own experience, I can confidently say that I have been commissioned more than I can confidently say that I have been called.

> *Therefore go and make disciples of all the nations, baptizing them in the name of the Father and of the Son and of the Holy Spirit, teaching them to observe everything that I have commanded you and I will be with you always, even to the end of the age. Amen.*

(Matt. 28:19–20 NIV)

As followers of Christ, we have all been commissioned to "Go." And the beautiful thing is that He does not send us alone, but He sends us with His helping hand through the Holy Spirit. The Scriptures indicate no matter what our job title, location, age, ethnicity, gender, or color is, we can be assured that we are all commissioned to *go* with special instructions.

1.   Make *Disciples;*

2.   Baptize in the name of *the Father, the Son, the Holy Spirit; and*

3.   Teach *God's Word.*

And to add, He did not commission us without the promise of, "*always being there with us,*" when we are in alignment with His instructions.

Where He has commissioned us to go is the place where purpose resides. Leaders are commissioned and placed in areas to fill in where there is a need. To name a few: Adam was placed in the Garden; Joseph was placed in Pharaoh's palace; Esther was placed in the king's palace for "such a time as this"; and David was placed in battle. This command does not require titles or positions but demands your willingness and obedience to His will for spreading the Good News. It is important to highlight that before we go to the place where purpose resides, we must take these commissions seriously within our own lives. A person who has been well-equipped will be prepared to *make disciples.* A person that has been baptized in the Father, the Son, and the Holy Spirit will be *equipped to baptize.* A person who has been taught the Word of God will be a *greater teacher.* A person who has been soaked in God's presence has the ability to carry God's manifestation everywhere they go as ambassadors of Christ.

For years, I have battled, trying to understand if my purpose was connected to the church buildings, ministry jobs, secular jobs, or owning my own businesses as an entrepreneur. At one point, I began to become so worried that if I wasn't pursuing certain careers, my purpose would be misaligned with my calling. We can be sure that purpose is connected to His commission to "go" and to the promise of His presence with us always everywhere we go. God's presence is all-consuming and all-present, meaning wherever you are commissioned to go, He is already there, waiting for you to move obediently. How awesome it would be if we had people in all different professions focusing on Matthew 28:19–20! The gospel would, in turn, reach every nation and the entire world, not by the ministers but by the common men and women who have been qualified not by their education but by the commission to "Go." Carrying God's presence alone can minister to an entire community of people that are desperate to know more of the Good News.

When I was five-years old, I began playing sports: basketball, football, and track were the three that I fell in love with —one sport for each season to keep me on my feet and out of the streets. As I began to excel and do well in these sports, I remember developing the mind-set that playing sports was my calling, so I imagined my life with sports forever. Throwing touchdown passes, making game-winning baskets, and running a guy down from behind in the 400-meter dash fed my passion for athletics. My parents would push for excellence, and my coaches would tell me that I could one day make a lot of money and provide for my family. Although I'm sure all the adults in my life meant well, it's important that adults' investment in young people should always be focused on the holistic development and not just talents. Those are two different types of investment, as one is directed toward the heart and the other is directed toward performance.

As I mature, I realize it is so much easier living life without carrying the weight of others' expectations. The only guarantee in your position is that, at some point, your position will come to an end. And when it does, you will only have yourself to face in the mirror each time. Like many young people, I've fallen victim to holding on to a sense of false reality, thinking I would be in the position I envisioned when I was young. For the most part, I've accomplished a lot of my goals, and I've accomplished more than statistics would show for my entire life given my upbringing.

However, when it comes to the transition from sports, I've had a really hard time adjusting. Imagine that you have been playing the wrong position all your life. You are really a running back, but your coach placed you on the offensive line ; or you are a center on the basketball court, but your coach makes you the point guard ; or you are a sprinter in track, but your coach makes you run long distances. The odds are you will not be as successful in the wrong position. This could be a hinderance to your development and diminish the passion for your sport. You may even begin to believe in lies like, "I'm just not good enough," or, "Maybe this is not for me." Living a life filled with the wrong ambition and the wrong involvement can be similar to an experience of being in the wrong position. When your life focuses on the earthly positions and not on an awareness of godly purpose, you lose sight of eternity. A person who is working in an environment that does not produce positive eternal impact is in a dangerous position.

We should pursue our eternal purpose over temporary positions. It is always so important to gain our kingdom's perspective over worldly aspects. Our lives are meant to reflect God's glory (purpose) on Earth (position), instead of our own ambitions. "*What good is it for someone to gain the whole world, yet forfeit their soul.* (Mark 8:36 NIV)? Eternity is the kingdom of God promised to those who accept Jesus in their lives. Eternity comes with promises that will never fail you. The Bible says that heaven is paved with streets of gold, has mansions to live in, and is a place of eternal joy, with no more crying and weeping. Purpose must align with your eternal destination. A team aligns its goals, its game plans, and its efforts toward winning the championship in the end. Eternity in heaven is the greatest championship that we must look forward to experiencing someday soon. However, we must focus on living a more abundant life now as preparation for the end.

Are you eternity-minded? Do the decisions that you make today cause you to think about the eternal outcome associated with them? A former coach of mine, Jamal Powell, would always declare that each day was "the best day" of his life. As a young man, I could not truly fathom his daily perspective and was probably too immature to think to ask why. I only assumed that the best days in life were only associated with events, such as graduations, birthday parties, career opportunities, and anything worth celebrating. Coach Powell declared that each day was the best day of his life despite those things because he understands that each day is a precious gift from the Lord to represent His kingdom. To add to Coach Powell's perspective, each day we live is actually one day closer toward eternity .

Today, as Coach Powell endures the battle against stage-four cancer, I can finally say that I truly understand his eternity mind-set and kingdom perspective. Even in his weakest hours, he remains faithful to living the best day of his life, today. Even before he was faced with this new challenge, his foundation of faith is helping him to overcome. We can always expect that being eternal-minded will *"win favor and a good name in the sight of God and man"*(Prov. 3:4 NIV). Just like any other day, Coach Powell wakes up each morning experiencing the best day of his life.

Purpose Unlocks Eternity

Knowing your purpose has the ability to unlock the future, to unlock the gates of heaven for your destination when you die, and to unlock purpose over position from other lives. For example, the life of Dr. Martin Luther King Jr. helped unlock the future of equality for all people. Despite the pushback that he received during his life's work, all of his prayers, sacrifices, and actions have come to fruition. Now, I'll be the first to say we, as a people and a nation, have a long way to go, but Dr. Martin Luther King Jr., through the civil rights campaign, was able to create and demand change in the broken systems of racism. Nelson Mandela, a South African political activist, helped bring an end to apartheid and became a global advocate for human rights. Although he was sentenced to prison for twenty-seven years, he remained true to his stance of opposition to the apartheid regime. After his release from prison, he negotiated an end to apartheid and later became South Africa's first black president, serving from 1994 through 1999. These men were ordinary men who became extraordinary because they stayed true to their convictions! Their life's work unlocked many years of oppression, bondage, and captivity. They both invited God's presence and carried his authority with them as they became public speakers, unlocking eternal change in our communities across the globe.

Experience and Exposure

There is purpose in our experiences and our exposures. Experience and exposure can shape our mind-set, give us a different perspective, teach us necessary lessons, and help us to gain more knowledge and wisdom. You can experience the benefits of another culture on the basis of whom you are connected to. For example, my wife's best friend is from Senegal, West Africa. My wife was fortunate to visit Senegal for three months with her bestie during the summer break, when she was sixteen-years old. That experience was filled with three months so rich in culture that, although the trip happened over decade ago, she still reaps its benefits and lessons. Even to this day, my wife understands the basics of the Senegal Wolof language, dancing traditions, and other important cultural uniqueness .

One thing she valued most about West African culture, was the level of respect, joy, and love the family members openly display for one another. The parents are pleased with their kids, and the children honor their parents exceptionally well. Even in her youth, she was able to distinguish these major differences in culture. Not that other cultures do not value the same, but she experienced a level of intentionality that she had not experienced before. Each time she visits her best friend's home in Richmond, Virginia, my wife still feels the warm embrace of the Senegalese culture. Because she has been exposed to these values in culture, she desires to implement some of those same values in our home.

For anyone who is connected with Jesus Christ, our Lord and Savior, you get to reap the blessings and benefits of the kingdom of God. Exposure to Christ's teachings and His eternal mission for salvation will empower the believer to live full of purpose beyond locality. Even without ever stepping foot in heaven, God's Word declares we can be exposed to heaven on Earth. This is evident in the Lord's Prayer, when Jesus tells the disciples to pray, *"May your Kingdom come, your will be done, on Earth as it is in Heaven"* (Matt. 6:9 NIV). Jesus had come to bring the kingdom of God to men. He made it clear that things are different in the world than they are in His kingdom. It is only by the grace and connection to Jesus Christ that the world can have access to the kingdom of God. When we come to learn that our citizenship pledges itself to the kingdom of God, we as believers begin to reap the benefits of our position on Earth. It's important that we begin to adopt the custom of the kingdom so that others will experience the glory of God's kingdom attached to our life's domain. In His kingdom, all citizens are provided for by the King.

Sometimes we can be exposed to different things without actually experiencing them. For example, we've been exposed to Jesus's teachings through His Word. Although today, we've never seen Jesus physically, we know that He exists, that He performs miraculous signs and wonders, and that He is the most recognized evangelist the world has ever seen and so much more. Because we've been exposed to his teachings, we still have the benefit of experiencing Him in the current day. We get to have a relationship with Jesus Christ because we've been exposed to Him through His Word, and we experience Him daily through encounters with the Holy Spirit. Ultimately, what we realize is that our experience and exposure helps us to live beyond the natural.

The Walk of the Cross

Just for a moment, imagine with me the scene during Jesus's final moments on Earth before His crucifixion. The people made a mockery of Him being a king by clothing Him in a scarlet robe and a crown of thorns that pierced into his skull. The fatigue of the journey while carrying the very cross He would later be nailed to. According to the gospel accounts in Matthew (27:32), Mark (15:21), and Luke (23:26), the Romans instructed Simon of Cyrene to assist Jesus with carrying the cross because of the physical breakdown of His body. The people along the sidelines only screamed mockery into His ear and slandered His name. Some descriptions detail that people even spat on Him as He endured the walk. Jesus's walk toward the place where he was crucified reads as if it was performed in slow motion and as if it were taking forever for Him to reach His final destination. And to keep things in perspective, this walk took place after Jesus had already received lashes by the Roman officers.

I often wonder about Jesus's mind-set in the final moments before His death, and the humility it must have taken to know that He had the power and the authority to stop the horrendous acts. Although we cannot conclude His exact mind-set, we do know that Jesus positioned himself to be in total alignment with His eternal purpose to endure the cross and to defeat death forever. His purpose was to provide salvation to the entire world. The cross is a representation of the sacrifice that Jesus endured in order to fulfill His life's mission. Sometimes living in purpose is not always fun, convenient, or enjoyable, and although it may sound a bit discouraging, it is the truth. In order to embrace the purpose, we must embrace the walk of purpose within our earthly positions. There is a level of sacrifice associated with your daily walk of life. What is hard in your life right now? Are you walking forward, or are you stuck in one position? Are you acting in faith, or are you acting out of fear? What does your current walk with the Lord look like in this moment?

It is equally important to have reverence for God and His willingness to save a fallen humanity. Our purpose didn't begin when we arrived on Earth; it began at the beginning of time. Jesus carried the weight of sin from generation to generation. From the very beginning with Adam and Eve being deceived by the serpent, Jesus paid the price for us all. The cross is purposeful to the Christian faith, despite the humiliation that it was used for. After Jesus was positioned on the cross for death, he took in his final breath and spoke his final words: "*Tetelestai*," which means, in New Testament Greek, "It is finished." When you come to the end of your life, will you live in tears of regret, or will you reflect on a life that is finished? Of course, we cannot accurately answer that, since we can't predict the future, but every day you wake up, you have a choice to make it the best day of your life. Through all the good and even all the bad, your position in life does not dictate your ultimate purpose. Just keep on walking, no matter how hard the road gets. Jesus has already declared, "*Tetelestai*." So don't give up and don't give in, until He says that your destiny and your purposes in life are *finished*!

Author's Motivation: W. I. S. E.

"Those who are *wise* will shine like the brightness of the heavens, and those who lead many to righteousness, like the stars for ever and ever." (Dan. 12:3 NIV). *When I think of the word* wise, *I think of the acronym* Work In Silent Excellence! *Sometimes fulfilling purpose can be lonely, trying, and unmotivating at times, but having a strong work ethic behind the scenes is typically a wise approach. Before an elite athlete publicly displays their talent in competition, he or she must put in a countless amount of hours behind the scenes practicing.* Working In Silent Excellence *does not discredit inviting others to journey alongside you, but it is an intentional focus on protecting the integrity of the things that you are working to accomplish.*

For example, as a free agent professional football player, you never quite know when your opportunity will arrive. In 2016, after recovering from injury, I had a great opportunity to participate in rookie minicamp with the New York Giants and later suited up for the Saskatchewan Roughriders of the Canadian Football League. In 2019, I was blessed with the opportunity to participate in the Your Call Football professional spring league. Even after a three-year gap of not playing, I embraced the Work In Silent Excellence *motto and ended up being the unanimous MVP of the four-game series. As a result of my performance, the next year I had an opportunity to suit up to play in the XFL—DC Defenders and Dallas Team Nine. This was by far the most promising professional football opportunity for my skill set but due to the Global COVID-19 pandemic, the league was forced to end all operations. Though my professional football playing days may be uncertain, I am still committed to* working in silent excellence.

W.I.S.E goes against today's culture with the advancement of social media because society has embraced being able to be involved in everyone's business. Social media allows the platform for individuals to now have a say in the process in another person's life journey, which could be both a really good or really bad thing. There is true wisdom however, when we intentionally work toward achieving a goal without the desire of being seen. A person that operates in excellence does not need the approval of man but rather the embrace of God. Silence is not shutting God out, but instead, it eliminates the noise around us to create space for His voice to clearly be heard. I urge you to be WISE in your endeavors!

CHAPTER 8

FAITH AND FORGIVENESS

A re you listening to God in this season? Has your faith been rocked by a certain person, group, or event that has happened recently? I know for many the hardships of the 2020 COVID-19 pandemic or the on-going conversation on racial division continue to plague communities of color. Even as a man of faith, I could always use a boost of Good News. The Bible declares in Romans 10:17 (NKJV) that *"faith comes by hearing, and hearing by the Word of God."* Listening to God's Word is the key to our faith growing. Just as a flock of sheep knows the voice of its shepherd, so our ears must be glued to His voice and His kingdom's sound. If sheep, who are scientifically known to be one of the most unintelligent animals on the Earth, can know their master's voice, then we, who are created in intelligence can develop an ear to know God's voice. We must be aware of His voice by hearing the Word of God.

Evaluate your faith journey with God. Are you relying on what man says or listening to the Word of God? In the beginning years of my life, the only time that I dived into God's Word was in church on Sundays. However, I realized that I was not learning to recognize the sound of His voice without the presence of man. Pastors and teachers of the Word of God should always be respected.

However, it wasn't until I began to study the Word for myself outside of just Sundays that I experienced God's fruitfulness. We must build a spiritual discipline to exercise our faith by diving into His Word and by hearing His Word.

God created humanity to display faith among those in His land. God created us all with muscles as the outer covering of our flesh. Your muscles become stronger when you exercise them. If you desired to grow your arm strength, you begin to focus on exercises for that particular muscle group. Studying God's Word is essential for your life to grow in His kingdom's knowledge and wisdom in order to grow your faith. It is also essential training for your soul and for how you walk with the Lord throughout your life's journey.

Faith and forgiveness are directly in alignment with your growth in the Lord. Faith cannot grow when you operate in unforgiveness. In fact, it is impossible to grow in faith when you harbor unforgiveness in the depths of your hearts. Numerous scientific studies confirm that forgiveness leads to better physical and mental health outcomes. The mental component is something that we cannot see, which leads us to believe that our faith in a spiritual Creator can be affected as well. Relationships, friendships, and business partnerships can be restored through our forgiveness. Forgiveness has the unique ability to bring loved ones back together and to make enemies come together in unity. Forgiveness allows faith to be restored. Do not allow unforgiveness to halt your faith journey. In order to experience all the freedom that God has purposed for your life, you must position yourself to not only love others but also to exercise your faith through forgiving others. It's also important to note that faith is not just a one-time investment but a daily operation for the believer to embrace. This is evident by Jesus's answer to Peter's question about how many times he needed to forgive. *"Then Peter came to Jesus and asked, 'Lord, how many times shall I forgive my brother or sister who sins against me? Up to seven times?' Jesus answered, 'I tell you, not seven times, but seventy-seven times'"* (Matt. 18:21, 22).

The Weight of Unforgiveness

One of the hardest but most necessary films to watch, in my opinion, is a documentary series on Netflix entitled, *When They See Us*. It is based on a true event, popularly called, "The Central Park Five," which took place in Central Park in Manhattan. Although it was one of the most painful films that I've ever watched, I gained some deep revelation about the unfortunate tragedies that many people face on a daily basis. These five teenaged lives changed forever, after they were sentenced five-to-thirteen years in prison for a horrendous crime they did not commit. After they were pronounced guilty and were given their sentences in the courtroom, they felt numb, stabbed in the throat, and their lives were completely over. They were so young and innocent, but they were forced to mature before their time. I cannot even imagine what these young men must have gone through mentally, emotionally, and physically .

Years later, one of the men opened up about his struggles in life and about how he never forgave his father for not being there for him in his time of need. At just fourteen years old, he was interrogated by the police during a session when they encouraged him to lie about the crime scene, a lie that would ultimately place him behind bars. The young man didn't want anything to do with this wickedness, but after a conversation with his father, he was told to do and to say anything that the police officers wanted him to say in order to increase his chances of clearing his name from the conviction. Hoping that his son would be cleared, his father forced him to say exactly what the police officers wanted him to say: he lied about the other boys' involvement in this famous case about "The Central Park Five." He never forgave his father for this life-changing event.

The forgiveness process can be difficult at times, especially when it has changed many dynamics of your life. I am praying that, one day, this man will be able to forgive his father, even if he feels that his father doesn't deserve forgiveness. There is something that happens to the human emotions when we decide to let go of the built-up pain, anger, and resentment that we have toward someone else. When you have any opportunity to release unforgiveness you begin to think better, you grieve better, and you live better. It sometimes feels unfair and is never an easy process, but somehow those seem to be the places where God shows himself sovereign and true. That person may not deserve to be forgiven, but you deserve to be free from the bondage. However, it is certainly easier said than done.

PAUSE MOMENT: Let's take a second to reflect on this topic.

Here is a great place to take a break from reading, take a moment to address the unforgiveness in your heart toward someone, and invite God into the forgiveness process in your heart. Remember, forgiveness has more to do with your spiritual health than it does with anything else.

Forgiving My Father

My earliest memories of my father can be summed up by cocaine abuse, jail time, and complete absence from my life. There was this one corner store nearby where all the drug addicts seemed to gather. My mother and I would stop at this store to grab some snacks before dropping me off at the barbershop right next to it. On many of our trips, I would often see my father standing at the door, asking for spare change, looking for drugs, and doing whatever else addicts do. My father was so strung out that his body features looked fragile and weak. One time, I remember that we walked right past each other, like complete strangers. He saw me, and I saw him, but neither of us made any effort to greet each other like a normal father and son would do. I was about ten years old and mature enough to understand that something was odd about my encounters with this man, whose surname, Lee, I share. So many questions, uncertainty, and misunderstanding.

My father was sentenced to prison while I was in high school. He spent nine years in the penitentiary. Out of all of the unlikeliest places, behind bars is where our true relationship began —over the phone, of course. He reached out to me during my college days. At the time, I was a college student at Georgia Tech, and my athletic accomplishments, up to that point, gave me a huge shield of protection. As you might imagine, I was a bit skeptical of the motive and timing of his call. I began to feel as if there were some hidden reason he chose now to start reaching out. I also was very fortunate to grow up with my loving (step) father, which eased the burden of not having a relationship with my biological father.

I could have had lots of bitterness in my heart toward my father and could have chosen to ignore his request to build a relationship. Although I wasn't quite sure if our conversation would produce much of a relationship at all, I was at least willing to give it a try. My trying ultimately resulted in forgiving him for his faults, past, and not being in my life at all up until that moment. What helped me to embrace our relationship was not embracing him as my father but embracing him as my brother in Christ who was overcoming his past life of addictions. That perspective brought a major shift in the healing process. It also helped with the awkwardness of talking to a complete stranger who was half responsible for my existence on Earth. After my divine perspective shift, it was now my assignment, my mission, and my ministry to reconcile with my father. Today, we have a growing relationship, and I am proud to consider him a father and brother in Christ. Perhaps for you, you might have to look beyond a person's mistakes and treat them as if they were your own sibling who just needs a helping hand. At the time, it was so much easier for me to forgive my struggling brother than to make excuses for my absent father.

Ministry of Reconciliation

What does forgiveness look like to Christ? He has not only called us to reconcile, but He has also placed the ministry of reconciliation on each person's agenda. Forgiveness and reconciliation, to Christ, is putting His life on the line for the sinner even when He is not accepted by the very people He is on the mission to save. Jesus, who is God in the flesh, cares deeply about His wonderful creation in mankind and has even prepared a place for eternity for all humans. But, first, you must dedicate your life to Christ by confessing with your mouth that Jesus is Lord. Another requirement to walk in purpose with Christ is forgiveness. Forgiveness is not an easy thing to do, and it can certainly be a controversial topic that distracts people from growing (see 2 Cor. 5:18).

The devil is the one behind all wickedness and sin. Yes, Adam and Eve decided to sin against God, but who was behind that? The devil. Yes, Judas sold Jesus out, but who was behind that? The devil. Yes, there are violent and horrific crimes each and every day in the world, but take a moment to consider the invisible spiritual forces that we cannot see that influence people to do some horrific things. When we examine human history, we were created good in the image of God, and it was not until that cunning devil showed up that we were deceived, and the perspective changed. In order to truly forgive, we must understand the forces behind the person's wickedness. Yes, all men should be held accountable for their actions, and we certainly can't go around solely blaming the devil for the humanity's wickedness, but we must recognize the forces behind all of this madness. However, the solution lies within the hands of the great Redeemer, the Lord and Savior, Jesus Christ. Jesus is able to see the soul of the person, the creation of the person, and the innocence of the person. He is able to forgive sin and thus see the purity that comes from a human life redeemed by our Savior, and not the persuasion of the devil. The enemy has a home that will be cursed forever, and humanity has a choice to perish in hell or to thrive in the eternity of heaven.

The energy that it takes to sustain an unforgiving heart is energy that can be channeled into other necessary areas of your life. I remember that, one time, my wife and I engaged in a heated disagreement that led to both of us competing in the silent treatment for days. Eventually, the anger that I once felt had gone away by the end of the day. I remember the frustration disappeared, too. I simply had no more energy left to keep up with the frown on my face. In fact, I remember thinking, *Why are we even mad at each other again?* As I forced myself to replay in my mind why I had been so upset, it felt almost like a choice. I was choosing to remember the situation all over again just so that I could remain upset .

Do I want to harbor these negative emotions again and again? Or, would it be best for me to channel my emotions and energy into forgiveness? We've later learned from situations like that, and now we know how to get over them for the most part. Forgiveness is so important to move forward to live a purposeful life. We must model Jesus's life and example to reach our eternal destination. I thank God for forgiving me for my wickedness, dirty thoughts, past sins, and future mistakes. Without Him, forgiveness wouldn't be practiced as much, and we would live in a world with absolutely no hope for a better future.

I know a lot of people who have gone through some things that are hard to even swallow or who have been exposed to things that have scarred them for life. I encourage you to take up whatever unforgiveness that you are holding on to, write it down on a piece of paper, start a fire in your backyard, burn the piece of paper in the fire, and let it all go in your own heart. Open up your mouth and pray to your heavenly Father. God can handle any situation in any circumstance. He is waiting for your next steps of forgiveness. No human can fix this issue that has been plaguing your heart, so give it all to the Lord. *"For if you forgive other people when they sin against you, your heavenly Father will also forgive you.* [15] *But if you do not forgive others their sins, your Father will not forgive your sins."* (Matt. 6:14–15 NIV)

When you release that paper into the fire and ultimately in the depths of your heart, not only is that person forgiven, but you are also forgiven. Forgiving others is a requirement for unlocking the gates of heaven and the right for God to forgive you. For those of us who have decided to forgive, God is proud of you as you walk in freedom toward purpose over position. You will even begin to have open conversation about the process of forgiveness as a testimony to others, which ministers to a person's heart even more deeply. A display of forgiveness is so much more powerful than negative emotions. But first, that can come only through the grace of God. Faith plus forgiveness equals God's gracious love for His people.

Author's Motivation: Spiritual Edge

When your back is against the wall and you feel all kinds of pressure, what is your edge? What is your motivation, or what keeps you strong? "Having an edge" is a sports term that is thrown around in locker rooms before competition in order to inspire athletes to play with passion or with a certain chip on their shoulders. As we endure the pains and trials through life, we must have an edge to continue to press through.

The Word of God can be used as a great motivation tool to encourage, inspire, and give a person a spiritual edge. One of those passages of Scripture comes from Jesus's final prayer. During His final moments, He prayed, "Father, forgive them for they know not what they do." Of course, nothing that I have ever been through can compare to the life of Jesus and His eternal sacrifices for humanity. But as we see Jesus as God, Father, Mentor, and Friend, quoting His Word will help transform our mind to refocus on the mission that

He has called us to. So whenever someone wronged you, we should train ourselves to say "Father, forgive them." Whenever someone persecutes our purpose, we must say to ourselves, "Father, forgive them for they know not what they do" (Luke 23:34 NIV).

What inside of Jesus made Him forgive the very people that had beaten and hanged Him to the point of death? His words, "Father, forgive them for they do not know" is the spiritual edge that we long for in our hearts for faith and forgiveness. How could a man who was wounded so severely forgive in the midst of taking His last breath? Compassion, love, and humility allowed Him to forgive. Jesus did not allow someone's current position of hate to hinder His one-of-a-kind love for humanity. Whenever one's skills are looked over or passed up for the promotion, instead of getting emotionally upset, operate in your spiritual discernment by carrying your spiritual edge. This edge gives you a new level of confidence to press forward, no matter what, with the assurance that God is with us. Not to mention, it is a healthy practice to release the unforgiveness in our heart toward another person.

CHAPTER 9

UNDEFEATED

We serve a God who is undefeated. Having an undefeated mindset takes extreme discipline and focus on the task at hand. Going undefeated is not easy, no matter what level of play. God, who is able and mighty, allows us to live an undefeated lifestyle, once we place our faith in Him. When we put our trust, our faith, and our lives in His hands, then there is nothing that can worry us away from His grace and salvation.

In high school, I was a part of a legendary state championship team, which went the entire season undefeated. The 2010 Hillside High Hornets, led by Head Coach Antonio King, were state champions with a perfect 16–0 record. I had no idea the impact of what winning the state championship would have on the entire Durham community. Because of poor academic performances among students at my high school, there were rumblings in the community about the possibility of Hillside High being shut down completely. However, alums from our school and the Durham community began to unite around the significant play of our football team. We football players had no idea that our team's success would influence decisions and impact the way other people would view our school.

What was unique about that season is that we had the leadership, the talent, the coaching, and the skill to have confidence that this year would be our year. So we came up with the motto, "All in 2010 16–0 State Champs." That was the mission and the vision that all of us in the locker room had tattooed on our hearts. We had a certain culture that we all truly believed in, and everyone was willing to abide by that standard of excellence. Throughout the preseason, we built a strong bond with one another and became not only teammates but also brothers. We rightfully called each other out, we got into blows, and we competed against each other in practice to maintain the integrity of our "*all in*" motto. We knew that if we went hard in practice, we were more than equipped to have the undefeated season that we hoped for. Our goal was set out to win the North Carolina 4A State Championship. So there were sixteen teams standing in the way of reaching our goal!

Going into each game with an undefeated mind-set is totally different from hoping to have an undefeated outcome. When you approach life with tenacity and joy every day, you are not worried about the results; instead, the results are a representation of your commitment to the mission. We expected to not only win the championship but that we would also not be beaten all season. If our efforts did not match our goals, then our coaches were not shy about letting us know how they felt. Our leaders would check the pulse of the team daily to identify any lack and begin to implement plans of actions. In the semifinals, we played against a really tough New Bern team that was equally matched up with our talents across the board. At halftime, we found ourselves losing for the first time all season long. Looking around at the pulse of the team at halftime was one of the most remarkable team settings that I've ever been a part of. In complete control of our emotions, everyone was calm as players gave reports on the opponents, while the coaches discussed their adjustments among each other. There was no panic in sight for our team. Not one single person had a defeated look on their face. This game was bigger than one person's emotions, but it was a sign that we had already come to know, that no matter what, we were going to find a way to win .

Before going out to the field that night, Dr. Phyllis Joyner came to speak to the team. She later became my spiritual mother and mentor as I was drawn to her authoritative demeanor and powerful display of confidence of God so evident in her life. Her message that night to the entire team was to be unstoppable. Toward the end of her message, she instructed the team, both coaches and players, to repeat the word *unstoppable*. Now imagine being in a crowded classroom with over fifty high school players and coaches shouting out at the top of their lungs, "Unstoppable" over and over again. It was electrifying. We must have said the word unstoppable enough for us to actually believe that we would be unstoppable .

In the midst of these big football players was this small elderly lady leading the charge of what would be an unstoppable second half for our football team's winning performance. We reminded ourselves of that pre-game message: "Who are the Hillside Hornets? Unstoppable! Who is offense? Unstoppable! Who is defense? Unstoppable! Who is special teams? Unstoppable! Who are the coaches? Unstoppable!" Those repeated words became our mind-set and the motivation that we needed in order to win the game. Though we faced some challenges in a close game, in the end we believed that we would come out victorious .

As children of God, let me remind you today that you are unstoppable. Though you may face some bumps along the way, your life in Christ is unstoppable. Your faith in God is unstoppable, and it empowers you to endure! Your divine purpose is unstoppable. With God all things are possible, and the Holy Spirit who lives in you and guides you is unstoppable.

That night, we won by a score of 14 to 6, to win our school's first division championship and to make our school's first appearance in the NC 4A State Championship game. My point is this: do not go through life cocky, but go through life confident. Do not take your position for granted, but let your position lead to a greater purpose. You were created to win and to live undefeated. And though you may experience both negatives and positives throughout your journey, in the end, you will win.

Pray the Word of God

In order for us to be connected to an undefeated God, we must embrace an undefeated prayer life. Prayer shifts our mentality to not focus on our ability but to focus on His divine glory. Prayer is, simply put, conversation with God. The Bible says in James 5:16 that *"the prayer of a righteous person is powerful and effective"* (James 5:16 NIV). Your prayer life has the potential to change a negative outcome into a positive outcome and a bad day into a good day. Do you truly believe that prayer changes things? I surely hope so, as I've personally seen the hand of God move in so many ways as a result of walking out my faith through prayer. There is no possible way to live an undefeated lifestyle if you do not fervently pray to the Lord. Prayer is not intended to only get you what you want or out of a tough situation but it is intended to invite God's divine presence into your provision.

Jeremiah 29:11 NIV, is one of my all-time favorite Scriptures in the Bible. While all Scripture are divinely effective, we tend to sometimes personally connect with some over others. For me this Scripture is one that I've built a personal bond with during my prayer time: *"For I know the plans I have for you,"* *declares the LORD, "plans to prosper you and not to harm you, plans to give you hope and a future."* God already has a plan, and his plan includes operating in purpose throughout your positions and overshadowing your possessions in the world. In studying His Word, we must continue to apply wisdom in our personal relationships. Jeremiah 29:11 has always been personally manifested in my life to empower me to walk in alignment with God's will. I often speak this verse out loud during moments of reflection, with my name inserted into it:

> *"For I know that my Father in heaven has good plans for Vad, plans to prosper Vad and not plans to harm Vad, but plans to give Vad hope and a future."*

The Word of God belongs in your prayer life to best remind you of who you are and whose you are. You are the Lord's creation, formed in His likeness and image, the *imago Dei*. You have legal, kingdom rights to personally cherish and apply His Word into your life. Moreover, your life's convictions should yearn to abide, to align, and to operate by His Word. Sometimes, we get caught up with very eloquent speeches, long-winded prayers, and big words to make ourselves feel better about who we are. God does not require that we speak on our own behalf, but simply, His Word alone will help us to live out purpose.

The more that we are in His Word, the more we began to look like Him, and the more we began to allow the Holy Spirit to work through us .

By owning Scripture in prayer, we begin to get in tune with His will and not our selfish desires. Prayer is a direct line of communication between you and the Father. Utilizing the voice of prayer is an invitation for God to enter into your heart. Your prayers have the ability to cover and influence territory. How awesome when we get to call on God, who is omnipresent, to meet us where we are, even when we are physically not together. The word *omnipresent* simply means that God is present everywhere at the same time. Through the Holy Spirit, God has given the believer unlimited access to Him at any moment, no matter the location. Though some Scripture may have been used for an appointed time, one can still be empowered by His Word, because purpose remains, even when positions in life change.

Safe Place

If I were to ask you, "Where is the safest place to be?" Most people would think about a physical location. But there is not quite one safe place that can provide an escape from challenges and oppositions. However, we should consider that the safest place for man to be is not in a physical sense but a spiritual sense —in God's presence. We can find comfort in this in Psalm 46:1–2 (NIRV): "*God is our safe place and our strength. He is always our help when we are in trouble. So we will not be afraid, even if the earth is shaken and the mountains fall into the center of the sea.*" His presence is the place where we find eternal joy that surpasses natural understanding, even in the midst of surrounding darkness. God is not limited to a specific location but is anywhere and everywhere His Holy Spirit resides. Consider these two Scriptures on this truth:

> *It is to your advantage that I go away, for if I do not go away, the Helper will not come to you. But if I depart, I will send him to you. (John 16:7 NKJV)*

> *And I will ask the Father, and he will give you another Helper, to be with you forever, even the Spirit of truth, whom the world cannot receive, because it neither*

sees him nor knows him. You know him, for he dwells with you and will be in you.
(John 14:16–18 ESV)

Do you have the helper living inside of you? Has the Holy Spirit made His home within you? Jesus promised that all who believe in Him and have a relationship with Him have access to the Helper. Who is this Helper? The Helper is the presence of God who lives on the inside of you. The Helper is the Holy Spirit who lives on the inside of you wherever you go. The Helper is the spirit who picks you up when you get knocked down. The Helper is the one who tells you to go down the righteous path, instead of the road of destruction. It is the Helper who helps you to respond to conflict with the Word of God and not quickly reacting with a fleshly tongue of emotions. The proof is in His Word. God has delivered man in the fire, has closed the mouth of lions, and has defeated giants in the face of opposition. Nothing is limited to a limitless God. When we seek God and His purpose for our lives, we ultimately seek to be in His presence. We must fight to spend time in our safe place, where every thought is welcomed for correction, every sin will be forgiven, and every tear shed will be collected.

The Power of the Holy Spirit

The Bible tells us to *pray with all kinds of prayers* (Eph. 6:18 NIV). Applying the Word of God to our prayer life is essential for us to align ourselves with the Holy Spirit and not our flesh. Jesus outlines prayer in Matthew 6:9–13, when his disciples were curious about how to pray effectively. His response was a direct order to pray in what we now refer to as the Lord's Prayer. Compared to the many eloquent prayers that I've heard from many religious leaders throughout my life, Jesus's prayer can almost seem too simple. Yet though his ideal for prayer may appear to be simple, it was efficiently impactful. The Lord's Prayer covers many areas of life that we need in order to refocus our spirit back to His kingdom .

His prayer places emphasis on having reverence for God the Father, implementing God's will on Earth, gratitude for the day, forgiveness for self and others, and strength to resist daily temptations. We must strive to implement these instructions in our daily walk with God. Prayer is not based on how many big words we use or how many Scriptures we can quote. Our prayer must not be influenced by human ideas alone but by the Holy Spirit and by these same characteristics highlighted by Jesus: reverence, will, gratitude, forgiveness, and strength. This is in no way to discourage or to discredit the way that we pray but all the more to highlight Jesus's instructions on how to pray. Ultimately, Jesus placed an emphasis on His kingdom's purpose to help us walk in fulfillment within our earthly positions. Our prayer life should always demand the kingdom's perspective and response.

Once a person receives Jesus Christ as their Lord and Savior, they are born again. That means that you are reconnected to God the Father, through Jesus the Son, and receive the gift of the Holy Spirit. While you are concealed by the Trinity, God gives the believer access to seek after other elements of prayer and spiritual guidance. There are many gifts from the Lord, and spiritual gifts are prevalent all throughout the New Testament. Although there are many different theologies on spiritual gifts, God's Word is very clear on its importance for advancing the gospel all throughout the world (see Acts 8:14–17).

As I've gained a personal relationship with the Lord through Scripture, I experienced the uniqueness and divine power of God through the Holy Spirit. I remember being a new believer when I had a powerful encounter of the Holy Spirit. Through the laying of hands, Apostle Louis Dickens, from Ghana, Africa, prophesied and prayed for me to receive the baptism of the Holy Spirit. It was one of the most powerful demonstrations and heavenly exchanges that I never knew I needed to advance my personal walk with the Lord. This is not an advertisement for spiritual gifts, but it is an endorsement to dwell in the power of the Holy Spirit. In our lives, we may not be able to obtain all of the many gifts of God, but we should yearn to experience the fullness of the Lord .

It's important that we do not close God up in a box and limit the power of God through the Holy Spirit that lives on the inside of us. We are called to aggressively (1 Cor. 14:1) explore all of who God is through the Holy Spirit who is alive in us so that we can do *even greater works*(see John 14:13). This is a part of who we are, as He gives us permission to be fully captivated by the signs, miracles, and the wonders even today. Apostle Paul, the writer of majority of the New Testament, tells us : I urge you to seek the gifts of the spirit to continue to *"advance your spiritual progress"* (1 Cor. 14:2–19). Just like these believers in the book of Acts, our hearts should be encouraged to desperately seek after God's divine power within our lives.

Gifts of God

In life, we determine what we do with the gifts that God has granted us. Jesus never wasted time in His life on Earth, and He never wastes any of His gifts. Gifts are blessings that we can't afford to disregard. We didn't have to earn them, and we didn't have to pay for them. The gifts came exclusively out of the heart of God for our good. Dr. Myles Munroe teaches that "when a person discovers there areas of gifting, they become a person a purpose ." For instance, children are gifts from God (see Ps. 127:3). Parents are assigned to lead their children well and to be great leaders in their lives. As a father to my children, I love to spoil them with good gifts. And when they ask for certain gifts, it is a honor and joy for me when I can provide them. In the same way, purpose is a divine and a one- of-kind gift from our heavenly Father !

At times, I have been guilty of not operating in the fullness of God by neglecting the gifts that He has given me. It's important to know that you are living in your purpose when your gifts are being stewarded well enough to glorify the Father. How well are you stewarding the gifts that God has birthed inside you? Do you wake up eager to operate in your gifts? Think about Christmas morning in the households of young people who celebrate the holiday. All the young people in the home wake up super excited in anticipation of opening their presents under the tree. How exciting would it be if we are just as eager and more excited of unraveling the gifts of God to live a life full of purpose?

Have you ever received a Christmas present but were too afraid to unwrap it, so you decided to give it back to the owner without even opening it? Of course not, because every gift is intended to be received with joy and gratitude. The purpose of presents is for you to unwrap them with eagerness. Suppose a gift was returned without being opened. I imagine that would not be a good feeling for the gift giver. As God's children, we can disappoint Him by not capitalizing on the gifts that He has given to us freely. Disobedience in handling the gifts that God has given to us in this life results in being led into darkness (see Matt. 25:14–30). Obeying God and becoming a good steward of His gifts is in our best interest to live an undefeated life.

What gifts or talents has God given you that you've ignored in the past or have been too afraid to unwrap? Is one of those gifts or talents writing, singing, teaching, dancing, acting, or building? Maybe it's a certain career that you were too afraid to go for. When life comes to an end and you stand before God's throne of judgment, we should be confident that we have served our gifts well and that they have been utilized in the way God has intended. God has blessed us all with unique gifts in our lives that are irrevocable and that helps guide us through our ultimate purpose (see Rom. 11:29). Your gift was built on the inside of you for His glory and your good.

Worry Less

God has a bed with your name on it, and He is preparing it for you. *"My Father's house has many rooms; if that were not so, would I have told you that I am going there to prepare a place for you"* (John 14:2 NIV)? With that truth in mind, as believers, why do we worry? Why do we live life afraid? And, why do we get so easily discouraged in pursuit of our purpose? There is no competition for a room in God's kingdom, so stop comparing yourself to your Instagram followers, Facebook network, and Twitter feed; instead, focus on the undefeated purpose that our undefeated God has given us to win in life.

In today's society, we tend to worry about anything and everything under the sun. To worry is to entertain defeat. For example, one of the things that I hear a lot is, "What if I'm wrong?" This is the type of doubt that is in the minds of those who are stepping out into the water on faith. Let's not make the same cycle of mistakes by focusing on doubt, rather than fixing our eyes to Jesus. When you do not take your shot, you allow fear to trap you in the deep pool of regret. But when you go for the win, you put yourself in position to win. You can never be wrong when you submit to the kingdom of God. Wrong is building an empire on Earth, hoping to make it last. Right is inheriting the kingdom dominion on Earth as it is in heaven .

We often derail our purpose by worrying about tomorrow's agenda or the next opportunity or next year's birthday celebration. Do yourself a favor, and take a moment to pray for deliverance from worry. Not once does the Bible tell us to worry about something, to stress about something, to get frustrated about something, or to figure something out on our own. God did not create human beings to live a life of worry but to live a life of purpose! God created humanity as the *imago Dei*, with dominion and rulership. The word *dominion* is derived from the Latin word, *dominium*, and is used in the Bible to mean that you "are in charge of" something or "rule" it. For example, God has dominion over the world. A king has dominion over his kingdom. In Genesis, chapter 2, God instructed Adam to have dominion over all the earth. Which means that you also have dominion over walking out your divine purpose! When you live with dominion, you will expose yourself to miracles, signs, and wonders; your mind-set will be transformed; and you will live a life free from worry.

It is wise to not allow others' defeated mind-set to hinder your undefeated quest. What others think about you will not help you reach new heights; instead, it will propel you into the opposite direction of a successful season. Your purpose is not for everyone to agree with or even to follow. You may have to pass up on opportunities during your climb of success. It may not feel wise in the moment, compared to a worldly view. Sometimes it just feels more prudent to give up, and the older we become, the more society encourages us to stop dreaming. It feels wiser to live a life that gives no room to criticize. But you may have to pass up on certain relationships along the way because that person is going at a different pace than the pace God has you on or maybe it's not the right season. In the moment, you may feel cruel and a bit uncomfortable, but your purpose must rule over your emotions. You may have to take certain chances that may not mathematically add up, but anyone who follows God knows that His math scale is foreign to the world, anyway.

Wisdom comes from God, while agenda comes from man. Wisdom leads to purpose, while agenda leads to position. Wisdom leads to truth, while agenda leads to deception. Wisdom leads to confidence, while agenda leads to doubt. According to James 1:5 (NIV), *"If any of you lacks wisdom, you should ask God, who gives generously to all without finding fault, and it will be given to you."* It is important to ask for daily wisdom, and God will give it to you freely. Godly wisdom puts things into the right perspective, at the right time, and realigns your thoughts and actions to God's undefeated purpose for your life. What is more important for someone else may not be the same for you. Faith in your ability despite what others may see is what aligns purpose. You must be discerning about the advice you receive from others because it may not always be godly wisdom. Two plus two does not always equal four when it comes to this infinite, undefeated God.

Take a second to dismiss all the lies, the opinions, and the threats of others, including the "American Dream." Society's vision for success is to make most of self, but the goal of the gospel is to make much of God. Instead, focus on the purpose behind your next steps that you are building toward. You serve an undefeated God who cares deeply about your POP journey. You are on the winning team. God has never lost a battle, and He never will. There is no secret formula or clarity when you are discerning purpose. The only true clarity that you will receive is your next step of faith. Continue to take it one step at a time because each step is a representation of the process. The process of reaching the top makes the rewards that much greater.

Take Your Shot!

> *And suddenly, a woman who had a flow of blood for twelve years came from behind and touched the hem of His garment. [21] For she said to herself, "If only I may touch His garment, I shall be made well." [22] But Jesus turned around, and when He saw her He said, "Be of good cheer, daughter; your faith has made you well." And the woman was made well from that hour (Matt. 9: 20–22 NKJV).*

After years of misdiagnoses, broken promises from doctors, and concerns with her health because of the overflow of blood, this woman had one last hope: if only she could just touch the hem of Jesus's garment. She was so hopeful that God would change her situation, she shoved her way through the crowd toward Jesus. At the moment when her hand touched the hem of His garment, a supernatural exchange took place from heaven to Earth. Healing is a function of the kingdom that is a legal right to the kingdom's citizens.

I'm sure many would have been afraid to be as bold as she was. I'm sure others even thought that she was too unclean and that because of her condition, she was unworthy to approach Him. So, instead of asking for permission, she knew her legal rights as a kingdom citizen with a "I won't be defeated" attitude. Please brace yourself for another athletic reference. After twelve years of being told by doctors that there was no cure for her bleeding, she came within arms' reach of Jesus, and she took her shot! The athletic term, *taking your shot*, means "taking a chance." It can also be used as a secular saying for making the impossible possible. There is an inspirational quote out there that claims that "You miss 100 percent of the shots you do not take." This will forever be true. I admire this woman for taking her shot. Praise God that she did not settle for man's reports and let that stop her from accessing healing. The woman may have been dealing with this issue for twelve years, but she was never defeated. Her condition did not own her because she owned an undefeated mind-set. And this proves that our God cannot be defeated!

We no longer can afford to live life as the victim in defeat. Just like this woman, we must claim our legal citizenship to the kingdom of heaven, where we inherit His undefeated nature.

Author's Motivation: W.I.N.

If you have been reading along, then you should know that I love a good old acronym. One of those acronym's that I love come from the word win. *Any competitor understands the most important thing about competing is finding a way to win. Winning separates the good from the great and ultimately position themselves above the rest. The acronym that's made up from each letter in the word win, is* What's Important Now. *In order for a superhero to be great, he must not dwell on the past victories, but he must win the current battle at hand. In order for us to win in life, we must find meaning in our present moment and take advantage of what's important now. Harping on the past or flooding our minds with things that we hope will come makes us lose sight of what's important now. Each day, each hour, each minute, and each second is an intentional moment with God that we will never get back. So why not live life for the win? Playing for the win requires an intentional focus of taking full advantage of making every play count. As you and I matriculate through our own lives, we must embrace becoming a winner in the right-now moment. Finding meaning in our moments and taking advantage of each opportunity to love, to sow, to build, and to grow into a winning lifestyle.* Win the day! Win the battle! Win the test! *With the Lord on your side, you will* win.

CHAPTER 10

LOVE GOD
& PEOPLE

Love is the most essential part of life that every human being must have in order to live a purposeful life. A life that has no love is a lifeless soul that has lost sense of purpose. We were created out of love, to love, and to be loved. God does not make mistakes, and He had a purpose in mind when He formed us in our mother's womb.

God's love is unconditional, whether we deserve it or not. Through His love, we can also love unconditionally the things that He loves. Our purpose should in fact align with the very things that He cares about. God cares about protecting our life goals so much that He was willing to sacrifice His Son Jesus so that our purpose in life can have eternal impact. I am confident that serving my community has eternal impact. However, I find it very difficult to say the same about temporary positions that I've assumed in the past.

For God so loved the world that he gave his only begotten son, that whoever shall believe in him will have eternal life. (John 3:16 NIV). The first part of this Scripture highlights God's love for the world. When you love something or someone, it takes you to another level of commitment to that person or thing. In order to truly walk in purpose, you must have a certain level of love in order to reach a certain height of promise. Commitment and love are essential to a healthy marriage, a dynamic team, and self-edification. Without the two , somewhere along the journey, when the going gets tough, your foundation can be shattered with one mistake or with one obstacle.

The second part of this verse is that God gave His only begotten Son. When you love something or someone, you are willing to give your all, including yourself. I love my church community, so I give them my time and resources. I love my family, so I give them the earnings of my hard work to benefit their well-being. I love my body, so I am willing to give up my sleep time to get up at 5 a.m. to workout, train, and to get into the zone daily. What is it that you must give up out of love in order to obtain your purpose? God gave up His one and only Son, Jesus, so that we can have access to heaven through Jesus's sacrificial death and resurrection. Certainly, God is not asking us to give up our children as sacrifices, but He is asking us to give up something as an act of worship and evidence of our love. Maybe it's the video game or social media or alcohol or drugs. We have to give up something in order to gain full access to what we are purposed to do.

The end of John 3:16 reads *"that whoever shall believe in him, will have eternal life."* The third part of this Scripture highlights the word *believe* —not just believing in anything your heart desires but believing to one day enter the kingdom of God. When you believe, you operate in that belief, you think in that belief, you live in that belief, and you work toward that belief. Believing in Jesus is absolutely the greatest decision that one can make here on Earth. Next to that is believing in the purpose that God has made for you with the same fire and passion to obtain it. There is something special when you hear a teacher, a parent, or a coach look you in the eyes and utter the words, "I believe in you." Those words are important for every person in the world to hear. Belief in yourself is great, but someone else's belief in you shows great love.

Love Wins

At some point, almost every man is faced with the task of providing for the family. The difference between providing and protecting your purpose is love. I remember that, as a young man, what I loved to do was not aligning with providing for my family at the time. So I felt obligated to substitute what I loved for jobs that I generally disliked. Because of my responsibilities at home, I had to find a job that I was not necessarily passionate about but in hopes to provide. To be honest, I hated some of these jobs along the way. Every morning that I got up, I remember feeling like a walking zombie and totally out of purpose.

My attitude began to take a shift negatively. My mind begin to be affected with dry thoughts about my future. My parenting began to take a hit because I was not being fulfilled mentally. After learning that I could no longer be my best self, I decided that, in order to experience true freedom, I would have to pursue the things that I loved so that I would not cheat myself, my family or my purpose out of joy. Your purpose is like tending to a child. You must nurture it, study it, spend time with it, help develop it, and feed it every day with your hard work and dedication. Your purpose to be in fellowship with God demands attention, or else it will become wasted and underdeveloped. Some of the greatest positions are not even worth the risk if it results in negatively impacting your divine purpose.

One of my favorite Christian songs is titled "Echo," sung by the talented artist Tauren Wells. The chorus is what I find profound.

> When my mind says I'm not good enough,
> God, You're enough for me.
> I've decided I'm not giving up
> 'Cause You won't give up on me,
> You won't give up on me.
>
> Your love is holding on and it won't let go;
> I feel it breaking out like an echo.
> Your love is holding on and it won't let go.

God's love is always with us, and He won't ever let go. The singer does a great job of capturing our mind and the conversations that we intuitively have in our heads daily. As humans, we sometimes tend to talk ourselves into anxiety, depression, and fear. But knowing that God won't give up, offers us the necessary confidence to overcome the battles that we may endure. His love has been holding on since the creation of humanity. His love is holding on since the death and resurrection of Jesus. His love is holding on, and it won't let go, even to the very end of time.

The Love of a Mentor

Mentorship is love. It is less likely for you to give up or to give in with a mentor by your side. Mentors allow you to be exposed to the blind spots that you were not able to see before. In fact, as a result of great mentorship, I see movies differently, I see reading books differently, I see money differently, and I see life differently. Having a mentor is essential to achieving a purposeful life. Mentorship is like a cheat code for obtaining a successful life because he or she unlocks the maximum potential of a person's advancement. Mentors can help increase business sales and marketing strategies, can develop new skill sets, and enhance your overall level of thinking .

If you've ever watched a horse race, you would notice that these big horses can run at a speed that is absolutely remarkable and breathtaking. They can run up to a maximum speed of fifty-five miles per hour. In addition, horses have almost 360 peripheral vision. The good is that they can see everything around them; the bad is that they can see everything except what's ahead of them. People often fit them with blinders that prevent them from seeing what is beside or behind them. My favorite part about a horse race is when the final lap approaches, the jockey begins to motivate the horse to go to a new level of speed .

People, much like horses, sometimes require extra motivation and inspiration to go beyond the capacity that they could never imagine on their own. In life, we first need mentors to be the blinders that will help us to focus without distractions. Second, we need mentors to push us past our limitations to reach new goals, new dreams, and new heights. This helps us to gain access to a new level of experiences that can only be provided through the love of a mentor. Adversity oftentimes has a way of making people fold, but when there are mentors in place to counter that adversity, your chances of survival increases. It is wise to include mentors in every area of your life, even if it is just for accountability purposes. Mentors love with intentional perspective that only benefits you and not for personal gain. They may only be with you for a season, but they have the ability to have long-term impact that could potentially carry you all throughout life. As a life coach for many young people, I thoroughly enjoy the opportunity to mentor, but more importantly, I love to have the opportunity to be mentored.

For this, I am thankful for my spiritual mother, Phyllis Joyner, who has been the best example of Christ in my life so far that I strive to one day imitate. I strongly encourage having spiritual parents in your life. Ms. Joyner came into my life at the perfect time—when I transitioned from high school to college, from teenage years to manhood. I was your average teenage boy who cared more about sports and girls than the spiritual wisdom that she would present at times. But I was in desperate need for spiritual guidance, and Ms. Joyner's mentorship increased my spiritual awareness. She spent countless of hours with me, developing my spiritual maturity through prayer, fasting, and many glorious lessons.

You never really know what you need until you are in the midst of it, or when it's gone. She had a unique ability to challenge me spiritually and to build me up to become a model man with godly principles. She often spoke with authority and deep conviction that either brought me to my knees or brought tears down my face. I believe that God allows her many lessons to be the voice of reason when I am faced with decisions to make, even to this day. The amount of information that I received during our time of fellowship prepared me for future seasons to come. I pray that those who are hungry to grow in the Lord would find spiritual family like Ms. Joyner in your lives.

My football mentor, Steve Wilson, is also another very wise man who played football in the NFL for nine seasons, participated in three Superbowl appearances, and became a phenomenal head coach at both Howard and Texas Southern University. Throughout the 2016 NFL draft, Coach Wilson was there by my side to help prepare me for the next level. Mentorship offers perspective that you have not yet experienced to warn you, to prepare you, and to educate you about certain areas of life. If having a successful life is all that you want, then it is possible to do so without having a solid mentor. But if you want to limit the bumps and bruises along the way in success, then it is not a bad idea to include a mentor with exposure in your field.

"When is none of your business"—*Coach Wilson*

One of the biggest lessons that I've learned from Coach Wilson is that when you love something so much, you have to be willing to put in the work, even when the opportunity is not guaranteed to present itself. Coach Wilson's famous quote any time his athletes complain or get discouraged: "When is none of your business." In other words, Coach Wilson liked to prepare the person who has put in the work to not worry about when the opportunity will come but instead to have the faith to continue to put in the work. The only thing is that you have no idea when that opportunity will present itself. This word of encouragement is sometimes hard to grasp, but it is very vital to the pursuit of whatever you are pursuing. I had no idea when my professional football opportunity would come, but, for three off-seasons, Coach Wilson continued to mentor and train me while I kept grinding because "when" was, apparently, none of my business. If I would have spent time worrying about "when" after year one and decided to hang up the cleats, then I would have not had the opportunity to compete in the XFL. In fact, it was this mind-set that got me a chance to become one of only twenty quarterbacks in the world to participate in the 2020 XFL professional league after being removed from the game for a very long time. Throughout my career gap, I never stopped dreaming and putting in the work to actually play professional football. Although the XFL 2020 season was short-lived due to the COVID-19 pandemic that shut down the league's entire operations, I can honestly say that experience was credited as a result of a mentor believing in me.

I am fortunate for the opportunity to experience the fruit of Coach Wilson's favorite line: "When is none of your business." As I've gotten wiser over the years, I realize that one must acquire a level of love to keep this quotation near and dear to the heart. Without love, there is no way that you would want to continue to pursue something without the guarantee of that position to come. Although Coach Wilson wouldn't strike you as a religious man, God has a way of using him to preach a message of faith. Having faith to keep pressing on, believing even outside of the playing field that someday, *when would be my business*, because I'm no longer waiting for it to happen; I am now in the midst of it.

"What has been will be again, what has been done will be done again; there is nothing new under the sun." (Eccl. 1:9 NIV). This Scripture indicates that the very lesson that you are learning now has once been experienced before and will one day be experienced again. That is the exact reason why mentorship is so profound for the development of the human experience. Mentors can teach us things in the past, prepare us for what's to come, and teach us from lessons along the way. For me, Coach Wilson is more than just a football mentor; his principles have developed me into a better man.

When you love God, you will dedicate your life to Him, no matter what your position is. Jesus's position was living as a carpenter until it was His time to be elevated to fulfill His purpose as the living sacrifice. He presented himself to become a mentor to the disciples, and in turn, they turned the world upside down in a good way. Jesus's recorded words in the Bible still inspire and motivate us today, thousands of years later.

The Love of a Friend

My good friend, Treshawn, and I have been friends since the age of nine or ten years old. We practically grew up together as brothers! Many days, we would hang out, playing tackle football in the backyard, competing in video games, having conversations about the future, and doing all the stuff that friends usually do together. We shared dreams of one day playing football at the highest level, so we would push each other, encourage each other, and compete against each other to obtain greatness. The love of our friendship carries great memories of our young lives. However, one day during our junior year in high school, our friendship took a rocky hit .

Like most teenagers, we both began to explore and discover both the good and bad ways of life. Treshawn and I began to establish new friendships with peers with two different lifestyles. Eventually, our friendship tanked; we did not communicate any longer, we no longer discussed anything, and we were not even being able to be in the same space. As the year went on, despite our differences, both Treshawn and I obtained full Division I football scholarships, as we set out to do since our Durham Eagle/Pop Warner playing days. However, Treshawn was not an NCAA qualifier because of his low GPA academic standings. As a friend and brother, despite our disputes, it was hard to see my childhood best friend not being able to act on the dream that we both dreamed together.

One of my favorite Scriptures about friendship is found in Proverbs 18:24 : *"There are friends who destroy each other, but a real friend sticks closer than a brother."* The climb to success sometimes requires losing people along the way. After high school, Treshawn did all he could to keep the dream alive by heading to junior college to improve his academics. Three years later, Treshawn willed his way to graduate with his associate's degree from junior college. This was a huge step for Treshawn, redefining success and for doors being opened again because of his fortitude. His actions began to align with his drive. And, therefore, it was only a matter of time to reclaim his opportunity.

During that same time, I was back on the recruiting scene; after three years of playing ball at Georgia Tech, I decided to transfer to another school. As a supportive friend, with Treshawn's eligibility in mind, I begin to make connections with the college coaches who were showing interest in me joining their program. Because I could only choose one school, I decided to entertain all the schools for the purpose to promote my buddy Treshawn's abilities. After only a few conversations with the coaching staff at Hampton University, they took interest and offered Treshawn a full athletic scholarship to play Division I football, which he gladly accepted. Treshawn went on to make a great impact on the field for two seasons, and, most important, he graduated with his bachelor's degree in liberal studies. Not only did he graduate from the prestigious Hampton University with his bachelor's degree, but, two years later, he received his master's degree in sports administration. God is so faithful, and His timing always links with the perfect opportunity.

Despite his struggles with academics in high school, Treshawn's purpose over position journey has helped him to live a life full of purpose. Now, as a well-educated man, someday, his knowledge from his associate's degree, his bachelor's degree, and his master's degree will all pay dividends. Many people wrote Treshawn off initially after not being eligible to go to college, let alone to graduate from college, but now this brother has earned three degrees before turning twenty-three years old. Stories like Treshawn's unorthodox journey helps us to see the beauty in God's restoration and love.

As Coach Wilson always says, "When is none of your business." You are more than what your current position has to say that you are. Jesus was positioned here on Earth, but He carried a heavenly purpose and anointing. He knew who He was, and He knew where He was going. He kept climbing, despite the challenges of life, so that we all could have great comeback stories like Treshawn's academic journey. Only this time, our prize will not lie in materialistic things like degrees or wealth, but it will be winning the prize of eternity in heaven.

I once heard a wise person say, "Evaluate your circle of friends, and I will be able to determine your future." Friends have the power to influence or to oppose the purpose that God has placed in your life. It is a necessity to have good friendships to maintain focus along the journey of life. My best friend Myer Krah, a Naval officer, a successful businessman, husband, and father, has been that friend who has stuck closer to me than a brother. Myer is an inspiration because of his love for others through humor and fun. I am totally inspired and motivated when I'm around Myer because he is one of the most gifted leaders that I've ever been around. I have personally never seen Myer have a bad day because his unique humor and joyful spirit gives him favor with just about anybody he comes in contact with. I love the times Myer and I share because we mostly share the same passions, goals, visions, and dreams that we are intentional about implementing to move our generation forward. One of our most gratifying accomplishments in life as of yet, was starting the *All In Scholarship Foundation* at Hillside High in 2012, during our freshman year in college. This scholarship fund raised by the community under our guidance has awarded many seniors at Hillside High to support their college academic endeavors. Without the two of us putting our heads together to merge our passions to build up people within our home community, I'm not sure we would have ever seen the fruits of the scholarship. I am so grateful that God would allow me to have a friendship that is so valuable and has become a pivotal part in my life. Myer is not just a friend, but he is what I consider a kingdom brother.

God allows certain people in your life for specific reasons and seasons to further enhance your purpose. I would like to strongly encourage you to invest in good friendships. Given the theme of the book, the two categories of friends that I offer you to consider is highlighting the differences between positional friendships and purposeful friendships.

Positional friendships are established solely on positions or locations, such as working the same job, being on the same team, or being a part of the same church community. Positional friendships are awesome for a moment in time, but they can be very hard to navigate once there is a change in circumstances. For instance, you will one day move to a different location, accept a new job, or try out a different church. When these changes do occur, the response of a positional friend will be very difficult to maintain the same level of connectivity as before. Ultimately, the transition could cause a huge drop off in the friendship.

Purposeful friendships is a true authentic connection between two or more individuals that does not need circumstances or similarities to maintain the connection. For example, Myer and I have never lived in the same state after graduating high school, but because of our commitment to a friendship of purpose, we have gotten even closer throughout the years.

While we are called to be good stewards of all friendships, it is wise that we have a good understanding of how to best serve and love others within our circle of influence. These two categories are designed to help us evaluate and acknowledge the foundation of friendships. Positional friendships can easily turn into purposeful friendships if both parties are committed and willing to not allow change in positions to negatively affect the normality of the friendship. We are products of the friendships that we make and the relationships that we build. As Dr. Dharius Daniels writes in his book *Relational Intelligence* , "our purpose requires people." We may never go as far as our dream; if we do not have a team. We need more than people who simply provide us company; we need people who will help us carry out our calling .

Scriptures indicate that friends will be by your side, even when family fails to do so. And when those moments of loneliness or pain or insecurities sprout, it takes a good friend to fill in the voids with love and encouragement. Even before establishing true authentic earthly friendships, it is wise that we get our understanding of kingdom friendships from Jesus. Jesus Christ has said with his own words that "*I no longer call you servants, because a servant does not know his master's business. Instead, I have called you friends, for everything that I learned from my Father I have made known to you*" (John 15:15 NIV). Praise God that we have a Friend in the supernatural that we can call on through the good and bad times. Having a friendship with Jesus Christ will guarantee that we live a life full of purpose. Friendship with Jesus means that we talk to Him, walk with Him, live with Him, connect with Him, partner with Him, and love Him daily. Jesus is the Friend that we all need in our corner who will confront us in wrongdoings, break bread with us at the table, celebrate with us when we have done well, and willing to protect us from harm's way. Each day that we live in purpose, we must call on Jesus as Lord but also view Him as our dear Friend.

Alpha and Omega

Every person has a beginning date (a birth date) and an ending date (a death date). For a long time in my life, death was a scary thought to consider. I'm not sure if it was because I was young or just too naïve to think that death is an unfortunate thing. It is natural for us to rejoice in God's beginnings, but we have a hard time accepting His endings. God declares in His Word that He is the Alpha and the Omega, which are the first and the last letters in the Greek alphabet and one of many names of God (see Rev. 22:13). For instance, when a baby is born, we celebrate and adjust life to welcome in this new bundle of joy. Also, when a person passes away, we typically have a homegoing service for the individual to celebrate the memory of that person's life on Earth. If we honor God for a new beginning on Earth, we should also honor God when a person has a new beginning in eternity with Him .

The reality is that our lives are guaranteed to have an end date. That process includes judgment before the throne of God, during which He shall welcome you into His eternal kingdom. He will also judge those who did not live a purposeful life to depart from His presence (see Matt. 7:21–23). If we remember, God's ultimate purpose for both the male and the female is for them to be in His presence. Consequently, there is a place for individuals who have chosen not to be in His presence. I've been to funerals of people who did not seem to live in purpose or who were not believers in Jesus, and I have also been to funerals of believers who seemed to live purposeful lives. Although God is the judge, I remember feeling a great peace of assurance in those who lived purposeful lives. What are you willing to do today to live in purpose, knowing that your life has an end date? I am in no way focusing on your death; rather, I am highlighting the importance of walking out your true identity, as God has already planned for your life.

In the end, as I write the final chapter of this book, I conclude that all those in life are in search of fulfilling their purpose. Purpose is not something that you find but something that is already predestined inside of you. In order to seek purpose, we must first seek the kingdom of God, having the faith to operate in God's presence every day. Jesus instructs us with the two greatest commandments as evidence of His love ; the first is to love God with all our heart and with all our soul and with all our minds. The second is to love our neighbor as ourselves. As you discern how to live a life full of purpose, continue to elevate your love for God and love for others. You will never go wrong with taking on the position of love.

Author's Motivation:
Endure, Obey, Maintain

"This means that God's Holy People endure persecution patiently, obeying His commands and maintaining their faith in Jesus Christ" (Rev. 14:12 NLT). *Only by the grace of God and His unconditional love can you fully grasp the concepts of enduring, obeying, and maintaining. These are three simple words, but they are very profound to the journey*

of purpose over position. Enduring persecution is the hardest thing about proclaiming the gospel, knowing that the world first hated Him, so it will hate you (John 15:18). But, through the love of Christ, believers are encouraged to endure instead of quitting or losing courage. When it comes to your purpose, you must endure seasons of failure or pain. Those seasons are guaranteed to come, especially if you are doing something right!

Obedience comes out of respect and love of whom we obey. Your level of love and respect dictates the amount of obedience that you are willing to give. If you truly respect God, then you will hear His voice. If you truly love God, then you will obey His commands. Obedience out of love is better than obedience out of fear. Bill Johnson once stated that " Obedience is not measured by your ability to obey laws and principles; rather, obedience is measured by our response to God's voice." Your purpose is rooted in your obedience to God. God can unlock new ideas, divine connections, and spiritual maturity through your obedience. If I had one word to describe God's love language, it would be obedience. Simply put, obeying God is putting your love into action.

Maintaining the faith can be incredibly difficult when you are faced with uncommon situations or positions. What does maintaining the faith look like from a homeless position, a divorce position, or an illness position? These are positions that could make it extremely difficult for you to maintain the faith, but holding on to the faith and maintaining it are the only hope that is worth giving your energy to. God does not work on our timing, but He does move when we display our faith. Giving up only leads to dry rivers, the opposite of purpose. Keep maintaining the fait, because faith is what makes God move.

ABOUT THE AUTHOR

Vad Lee is a native of Durham, North Carolina. As a scholar-student-athlete, his talents landed him at the Georgia Institute of Technology for three years and James Madison University from start to finish where he earned his bachelor's degree in Public Policy and Administration. Vad is the husband of the future Dr. Khayla Lee, who is finishing up her dental degree program at Howard University. Together, they are the parents of two precious daughters, Saraiah and Sinaiah Lee. Together they are also the authors of a dynamic cultural/diversity children's book titled *That's My Friend*. Vad has been able to leverage his platform as a professional athlete, a minister of the gospel, a public speaker, and leadership coach. Vad serves as an inspiration to major audiences around the world. His love for the Lord is what motivates him to "Go" and influence leaders to serve with greater assurance.